As we move onward through the 21st Century new leadership is emerging within the Republican party. The old guard, the likes of John McCain, Mitch McConnell and John Boehner, are aging and soon new faces will be leading the conservative movement forward.

Who are these lesser known lights who will in the coming years assume the political spotlight? Where do they come from? What are their views on the issues of our time? Terrorism? The Economy, Personal Liberty? And much, much more.

These things are best explored by examining the words of these future leaders directly. We are pleased, therefore, to present you this collection of quotations for your enjoyment and enlightenment.

21st Century

Republicans

James Buffington

ISBN-13:
978-1512365603

ISBN-10:
1512365602

Greg Abbott

America is ready for livable communities. America is ready for high-speed rail.

If I have to, I will use one challenge after another to dismantle governmental operations that I consider violations of the Constitution.

Americans get it. They're ready for some opportunities to have greener communities, to have cleaner communities, and to have transportation options that perhaps they haven't had in the past.

I typically start out almost every speech I give making some kind of joke about me being in a wheelchair.

America is sick and tired of spending hour upon hour sitting in their automobile trying to get to work, trying to get kids to school, trying to get to a doctor's appointment.

During my time as a judge, as a justice, and as attorney general, I've had one overarching goal, and that is a strict interpretation and application of the laws and the Constitution. I would be Madisonian.

You can look at the state of California, which is on a pathway to destruction because they expanded government too much, thinking that there would always be someone to pay for it.

Jeb Bush

Life teaches you that you need to make decisions in the right time - not too early, not too late.

Public education must be viewed from the lens of providing each child with the learning environment that best meets his or her needs. If we can send a low-income child to a parochial school, knowing that his odds of attending college will increase as a result, then that should be our mission.

Our children can achieve great things when we set high expectations for them.

There's a fine line between stubbornness and the positive side of that, which is dogged determination.

When businesses go through hard times, through down markets, what do they do is they challenge every basic assumption of how they operate. They innovate. They create disruption for a while that leads them to even greater heights when the economy turns around.

Great countries need to secure their border for national security purposes, for economic purposes and for rule of law purposes.

I don't think a party can aspire to be the majority party if it's the old white guy party.

I would say national security is work in progress.

As governor, I saw the link between economic prosperity and the ability to acquire knowledge.

I think Republicans really need to be disciplined, to stay focused on sustained economic growth.

Well, I think lower taxes and less regulation would actually promote growth.

Everything's viewed with a political lens in Washington, and that's just the nature of the beast, and it is what it is.

Leaders lead. They don't divide; they don't create a climate that is poisonous.

Low standards are a tactic that takes pressure off teachers' unions by accepting mediocrity and failure for kids.

Second-generation Hispanics marry non-Hispanics at a higher rate than second-generation Irish or Italians. Second-generation Hispanics' English language capability rates are higher than previous immigrant groups'.

We are stronger because we recognize that government isn't the sole answer to the most important questions, and we welcome community and faith based organizations as partners to serve the needs of Florida families.

Any time an elected official in the world we're in today that appears so dysfunctional challenges a core constituency not of their opponent but of their own political base, I think we should pause and give them credit.

If you believe, like I do, that the world is abundant with possibilities, then we need to make sure we build capacity so that everybody is successful or can be successful in the pursuit of their dreams - not the dreams of someone from government, but their own dreams.

It's important to build trust if you're trying to deal with big things. Big issues require everybody to get outside their comfort zone, and people are more willing to do so if they believe that their partner is sincere in their efforts. And the only way you can do that is to engage them on a personal level.

But without a caring society, without each citizen voluntarily accepting the weight of responsibility, government is destined to grow even larger, taking more of your money, burrowing deeper into your lives.

I'm happy to be helping people that are passionate about empowering parents for student learning.

You focus on the things that you can control, and that's what I'm doing.

If you could bring to me a majority of people to say that we're going to have $10 of spending cuts for $1 of revenue enhancement, put me in, coach.

I have never wavered from my intention to advance the cause of diversity in new and more effective ways.

I support high academic standards. Period.

There are people who believe in expanding the welfare state across the spectrum of races and ethnicities and creeds.

Teachers make a difference, and we would serve our students better by focusing on attracting and retaining the quality teachers by raising teacher pay.

I don't believe you outsource your convictions and principles to people.

I'd be wary of simple solutions to complex problems.

I'm getting nervous to be called a centrist. Breaking out in a rash.

If you have to deal with our friends at ICE, Immigration and Customs Enforcement, it's like a Kafka novel. Files just disappear.

Immigrants are more fertile.

Immigrants create an engine of economic prosperity.

The Common Core State Standards are more rigorous standards than the great majority of states had in place previously.

The GOP should be the GSP: the Grand Solutions Party. It should be about solutions, not talking points.

Traditional marriage is what should be sanctioned.

Way too many people believe Republicans are anti-immigrant, anti-woman, anti-science, anti-gay, anti-worker.

Being against other people's policies eventually puts you in a downward spiral. It's fine to be principled and oppose views that you don't agree with, but you also have to have an alternative.

If you had to pick the values that would be held dear to a broad number of Hispanic voters, access to opportunity would be a higher value than guarantee of security, particularly amongst the newly arrived, meaning the last 20 years.

Clearly if the United States' relationship with Cuba changed, which would require a regime change inside Cuba, if Cuba moved towards a more democratic approach to governance rather than this despotic rule of tyranny, if they moved towards the systems that have created more economic prosperity, then our immigration laws would change accordingly.

I envision presenting parents with a marketplace of school choices - public, private, parochial, charter, virtual, blended, and home education. They then can choose the model that best equips their children for success.

I have a voice: I want to share my beliefs about how the conservative movement and the Republican party can regain its footing, because we've lost our way.

If we don't empower families to be able to have a quality education, then their children - for the first time in American history, truly the first time - will not have the same economic opportunities.

States are free to modify the Common Core State Standards or adopt their own individual standards, because academic standards are the prerogative of the states.

We need to end the government monopoly in education by transferring power from bureaucracies and unions to families. The era of defining public education as allegiance to centralized school districts must end.

I think President Obama has used the bully pulpit as a way to attack capitalism.

I never felt comfortable with making political decisions based on whether, you know, it was the right thing to do in terms of a poll.

If more people were actively engaged in advocating their positions I think we'd have a better society.

I don't miss politics.

I miss being governor.

I think life is precious from beginning to end.

I want my voice to have purpose.

I'm a conservative - a practicing one. I'm not a talk-about-it one.

I've always believed that if you support reform or you support a particular idea that you ought to fund that idea first and not the system.

If I can help create an environment where the principles that I believe in can be implemented - to me, that's fulfilling.

Immigration is a gateway basically. It's a check-off point for Latino voters.

Immigration is as much about the American experience and the values we share, and a lot more about economics than it is about politics.

In a divided government, you can't just say, 'It's my way or the highway.'

In Washington, particularly, the loyal opposition has a job to be the opposition. But you can't stop there.

People are moping around and I think campaigns can be about lifting the spirits of the American people.

Right now people seem to be very tentative about the positive benefits of capitalism.

The fact that the U.S. is superior to all others allows for free commerce to take place.

There's a direct link between percentage of young people that are educated and how we live our lives.

Treating people fairly and with civility is not a bad thing... It would be good for our country if political leaders actually took that to heart.

I really think that elected officials should be focused on how you create sustained economic growth, how do you create jobs and all of these issues that made people - segments of our society believe are really important are diversions politically.

I get tired of hearing people, well-meaning people, talking about African-American kids or Hispanic kids as if they're all the same. Which isn't true. There is a very diverse group of people in both groups in terms of income, objectives in life, aspirations, cultural wants, habits, all the things that make us unique Americans.

If I decide to run for office again, it will be based on what I believe, and it will be based on my record. And that record was one of solving problems completely from a conservative prospective.

If I'm a conservative, I'll generally watch Fox. If someone's liberal, they'll generally watch MSNBC. They'll basically learn a set of facts that are completely distinct from one another. They'll get their views validated.

Never again can the Republican Party simply write off entire segments of our society because we assume our principles have limited appeal. They have broad appeal. We need to be larger than that.

The dual effect of high growth creating higher income that's taxed by government at all levels, combined with lessening demands placed on government that occurs during economic prosperity, is a worthy objective.

There are cultural reasons, economic competitiveness reasons. There are a lot of reasons why people are in poverty. The difference today is that increasingly they are in perpetual poverty.

You tell me which society is going to be the winner in this 21st Century: One that worries about how we feel or the one that worries about making sure that the next generation has the capacity to eat everybody's lunch.

Ben Carson

Through hard work, perseverance and a faith in God, you can live your dreams.

No matter how good you are at planning, the pressure never goes away. So I don't fight it. I feed off it. I turn pressure into motivation to do my best.

You have the ability to choose which way you want to go. You have to believe great things are going to happen in your life. Do everything you can - prepare, pray and achieve - to make it happen.

Here's a nation, one of the founding pillars was freedom of speech and freedom of expression. And yet, we have imposed upon people restrictions on what they can say, on what they can think. And the media is the largest proponent of this, crucifying people who say things really quite innocently.

It doesn't matter if you come from the inner city. People who fail in life are people who find lots of excuses. It's never too late for a person to recognize that they have potential in themselves.

The most important thing for me is having a relationship with God. To know that the owner, the creator of the universe loves you, sent His Son to die for your sins; that's very empowering. Knowing Him and knowing that He loves me gives me encouragement and confidence to move forward.

Those of us who believe in God and derive our sense of right and wrong and ethics from God's Word really have no difficulty whatsoever defining where our ethics come from. People who believe in survival of the fittest might have more difficulty deriving where their ethics come from. A lot of evolutionists are very ethical people.

The Roman Empire was very, very much like us. They lost their moral core, their sense of values in terms of who they were. And after all of those things converged together, they just went right down the tubes very quickly.

I started reading about people of great accomplishment... and it dawned on me suddenly that the person who has the most to do with what happens in your life is you.

I think one of the keys to leadership is recognizing that everybody has gifts and talents. A good leader will learn how to harness those gifts toward the same goal.

Quite frankly, having an uninformed populace works extremely well, particularly when you have a media that doesn't understand its responsibility and feels more like it's an arm of a political party. They can really take advantage of an uninformed populace.

There are a group of people who would like to silence everybody and have everybody go along to get along, but that's not going to be very helpful for us in the long run, in terms of solving our problems. And somebody has to be courageous enough to actually stand up to, you know, the bullies.

You don't have to be a brain surgeon to be a valuable person. You become valuable because of the knowledge that you have. And that doesn't mean you won't fail sometimes. The important thing is to keep trying.

We should be concerned not only about the health of individual patients, but also the health of our entire society.

I don't want my kids to grow up with no father like I did. I came to the conclusion a while ago that you can work until midnight and not be finished or you can work until 6 or 7 and not be finished. I decided I'd rather work until 6 or 7.

Intelligent people tend to talk about the facts. They don't sit around and call each other names. That's what you can find on a third grade playground.

I detest politics, to be honest with you. It's a cesspool. And I don't think I would fare well in that cesspool because I don't believe in political correctness and I certainly don't believe in dishonesty.

Evolution and creationism both require faith. It's just a matter of where you choose to place that faith.

I would like people to recognize in looking at my story that the person who has the most to do with what happens to you is you. It's not the environment, it's not the other people who were there trying to help you or trying to stop you. It's what you decide to do and how much effort you put behind it.

There is no job more important than parenting. This I believe.

There's no question that as science, knowledge and technology advance, that we will attempt to do more significant things. And there's no question that we will always have to temper those things with ethics.

We are more than just flesh and bones. There's a certain spiritual nature and something of the mind that we can't measure. We can't find it. With all our sophisticated equipment, we cannot monitor or define it, and yet it's there.

It's very important for people to know themselves and understand what their value system is, because if you don't know what your value system is, then you don't know what risks are worth taking and which ones are worth avoiding.

People all over the nation are starved for honesty and common sense.

Health care is one-sixth of our economy. If the government can control that, they can control just about everything. We need to understand what is going on, because there are much more economic models that can be used to give us good health care than what we have now.

If we can take young people who excel at the highest levels, put them on the same kind of pedestal as the all-state basketball player and the all-state football player, and begin to get the same kind of recognition, it will have a profound effect, and we are finding that it does.

There is no fulfillment in things whatsoever. And I think one of the reasons that depression reigns supreme amongst the rich and famous is some of them thought that maybe those things would bring them happiness. But what, in fact, does is having a cause, having a passion. And that's really what gives life's true meaning.

The mind controls so much of the body. We are much more than flesh and blood; we are complex systems. Patients do better when they have faith that they're going to do better. That's why I always tell my patients and their families not to neglect their prayers. There's nobody I don't say that to.

I have no problem whatsoever with allowing gay people to live as they please, as long as they don't try to impose their lifestyle on everyone else.

There is a tendency of people to try to make you believe only a few people are smart. As a brain surgeon, I know better than that.

A lot of people simply don't realize their potential because they're just so risk adverse. They just don't want to take the risk.

A lot of people simply don't realize their potential because they're just so risk adverse. They just don't want to take the risk.

Resist this war on God, freedom of religion and freedom of speech.

Marriage is a very sacred institution and should not be degraded by allowing every other type of relationship to be made equivalent to it.

There is so much potential out there in young people and they aren't getting the right information or being encouraged in the right ways. This is our duty as a society.

We need to understand that we are not each others' enemies in this country. And it is only the political class that derives its power by creating friction. It is only the media that derives its importance by creating friction... that uses every little thing to create this chasm between people. This is not who we are.

But, you know, we have these entrenched entities - and I'm talking about both Republicans and Democrats - who believe that when you're elected to office, you become some kind of member of the aristocracy, and that anyone who challenges you is attacking you and is unpatriotic. This is foolishness.

What we need to do in this PC world is forget about unanimity of speech and unanimity of thought and we need to concentrate on being respectful of those people with whom we disagree.

Education is a fundamental principle of what made America a success. We can't afford to throw any young people away.

God has opened many doors of opportunity throughout my lifetime, but I believe the greatest of those doors was allowing me to be born in the United States of America.

Don't let anyone turn you into a slave. You're a slave if you let the media tell you that sports and entertainment are more important than developing your brain.

You can't allow the forces of political correction to shut you up. I mean, why are people afraid to say, 'Merry Christmas?' Give me a break. If people don't like it, yeah, they can go do something else.

We're not planning for the future. If we continue to spend ourselves into oblivion, we are going to destroy this nation.

Illogical thinkers throw names and slurs around because they have no arguments with which to rebut their opponents. Rational people have to keep hammering their points home.

If you go and talk to most people, they mean well but they don't have much of a breadth on education, of knowledge of understanding what the real issues are and therefore they listen to pundits on television who tell them what they are supposed to think and they keep repeating that until pretty soon they say, 'Oh, well that must be true.'

Nobody is starving on the streets. We've always taken care of them. We take care of our own; we always have. It is not the government's responsibility.

I would prefer to just continue to speak about truth and to speak about what makes sense.

I believe that things are always going to work out, even if in the beginning it doesn't look like they are working out. I know in the long run they are going to work out, and it's going to be fine.

I have this feeling that as time goes on, we're not getting any more civilized, and we should be. We're still running around like the days of Genghis Khan. There are so many important, better things to do and we need to encourage people to reach into the brighter side of humanity and not encourage people to continue to glorify the darker side.

What you're saying is that 'I, the superior elite, will take care of you.' Why? Because, you see, that superior, elite group needs to feel superior and elite. And they can't be superior and elite unless you have a whole lot of people down there groveling around.

So you keep them down there by feeding them.

The key is to cut out the middleman and empower both doctor and patient with information about what things cost.

We live in a country that used to have a can-do attitude, and now we have a 'what-can-you-do-for-me?' attitude, and what I try to do is find ways that we can develop common ground.

Before this country came on the scene, for thousands of years people did things the same way. Within 200 years of the advent of this nation, men were walking on the moon, and I want us to recognize this is the kind of people that we are. We're creative with a lot of ingenuity and a lot of energy.

Our schools too often want to shut people up so they can't talk about real solutions. People who think differently tend to clam up because they think something is wrong with their ideas.

This is a country for, of, and by the people not for, of, and by the government. If we turn it over to them we cannot complain about what they're doing because this is a natural course of men and we have to hold their feet to the fire.

There's a certain spiritual nature and something of the mind that we can't measure. We can't find it. With all our sophisticated equipment, we cannot monitor or define it, and yet it's there.

We need to find ways to elevate the expectations, particularly of those individuals who may start off on a lower socioeconomic rung, who might be seen as disadvantaged. But, you know, the reason I say be seen as disadvantaged, it's because life is so short, and there's so much that can change.

Every person is endowed with God-given abilities, and we must cultivate every ounce of talent we have in order to maintain our pinnacle position in the world.

People spending more of their own money on routine health care would make the system more competitive and transparent and restore the confidence between the patients and the doctors without government rationing.

Well, I say that the most important job you can possibly have is raising a child, and it needs to be treated that way. You have to show them, rather than just talk to them.

I want the government to provide the military so we don't get invaded by somebody and destroyed. I want the government to provide the roads so I can get from point A to B. In terms of taking care of my day to day needs, I want to do that myself. I want my community to do that.

You're going to be much less likely to point the finger at somebody and create a huge brouhaha when it wasn't necessary if you had stopped and asked yourself, 'Could I have done things to prevent this situation?'

You know, I'm a physician. I like to diagnose things. And, you know, I've diagnosed some pretty, pretty significant issues that I think a lot of people resonate with.

Let's let everybody believe what they want to believe. And that means, P.C. police, don't you be coming down on people who believe in God and who believe in Jesus.

With everything that is complex, we learn. If you don't learn, then it's an utter and abject failure. If you do learn, and you're able to apply that to the next situation, then you take away a measure of success.

Our children need to see and hear about more black role models in many fields so they can make better choices.

So after a while, if people won't accept your excuses, you stop looking for them.

Corporations are not in business to be social-welfare organizations; they are there to make money.

I could easily have decided that life was cruel, that being black meant everything was stacked against me.

Economics is not brain surgery.

The P.C. police are out in force at all times... We've reached a point where people are actually afraid to talk about what they want to say.

There's absolutely no reason at all that physicians, scientists, shouldn't be involved in things that affect all of us.

We have much more in common with other people than we have apart.

And I've always said, 'If two people think the same thing about everything, one of them isn't necessary.' We need to be able to understand that if we're going to make real progress.

Chris Christie

And the greatest lesson that mom ever taught me though was this one. She told me there would be times in your life when you have to choose between being loved and being respected. Now she said to always pick being respected.

Today, the biggest challenge we must meet is the one we present to ourselves. To not become a nation that places entitlement ahead of accomplishment. To not become a country that places comfortable lies ahead of difficult truths. To not become a people that thinks so little of ourselves that we demand no sacrifice from each other.

One state retiree, 49 years old, paid, over the course of his entire career, a total of $124,000 towards his retirement pension and health benefits. What will we pay him? $3.3 million in pension payments over his life and nearly $500,000 for health care benefits - a total of $3.8m on a $120,000 investment.

Our state is in crisis. Our people are hurting. Now is the time when we all must resist the traditional, selfish call to protect your own turf at the cost of our state. It is time to leave the corner, join the sacrifice, come to the center of the room and be part of the solution.

You know, at some point there has to be parity. There has to be parity between what is happening in the real world, and what is happening in the public sector world.

I believe we have become paralyzed, paralyzed by our desire to be loved. Now our founding fathers had the wisdom to know that social acceptance and popularity were fleeing, and that this country's principles needed to be rooted in strengths greater than the passions and the emotions of the times.

I know we can fix our problems. When there are people in the room who care more about doing the job they were elected to do than they worry about winning reelection, it is possible to work together, achieve principal compromise, and get results for the people who give us these jobs in the first place.

I don't compromise my principles for politics.

The job of a leader, the job of a governor, the job of a president, is to get the people in the room and bang enough heads together and rub enough arms and cajole enough to have them put the country and the state's greater interest ahead of their own personal partisan interest. That's what we did in New Jersey and that's the model for America.

If I missed my moment, I missed my moment. I mean, I wasn't pining to be president of the United States.

Well, let me tell you, after three years of Obama, we are hopeless and changeless, and we need Mitt Romney to bring us back, to bring America back.

Insisting that we must tax and take and demonize those who have already achieved the American Dream. That may turn out to be a good re-election strategy for President Obama, but is a demoralizing message for America.

The three top issues have to be restoring jobs and private sector job growth to our country, getting the entitlement mess under control, and restoring back to our country a sense of self-confidence that Americans can achieve whatever we want to achieve.

The truth was you can't continue to spend the kind of money our spending on all these entitlement programs. I think we need more people in public life who are willing to say, no, we can't afford certain things. No, we can't do certain things.

We believe - we believe that, if we tell the people the truth, that they will act bigger than the pettiness we see in Washington, D.C. We believe it is possible to forge bipartisan compromise, and stand up for our conservative principles.

If you're sick, take your sick day. If you don't take your sick day, know what your reward is? You weren't sick - that was the reward.

This country pays a price whenever our economy fails to deliver rising living standards to our citizens - which is exactly what has been the case for years now. We pay a price when our political system cannot come together and agree on the difficult but necessary steps to rein in entitlement spending or reform our tax system.

You know, I think what the American people want more than anything else right now is someone who's just going to look them in the eye and tell them the truth, even some truths that they don't like. And - but they have to believe the person's speaking from their heart and are authentic.

We pay a price when special interests win out over the collective national interest.

Given my last position, that I was the first U.S attorney post 9/11 in New Jersey, I understand acutely the pain and sorrow and upset of the family members who lost loved ones that day at the hands of radical Muslim extremists. And their sensitivities and concerns have to be taken into account.

But our leaders of today have decided it's more important to be popular, to say and do what's easy, and say yes rather than to say no, when no is what is required.

If we make the tough decisions now, we will be one year ahead of 80 percent of the states in the race to economic growth. If we fail to act, we will fall even further behind... by going first, we can become first.

If anybody ran a business like that they would be out of business quickly, and Barack Obama's leadership is driving this business, the United States of America, toward a fiscal cliff.

Higher taxes is the road to ruin. We must and we will shrink our government, and that means making some tough choices, tightening our belts.

Everyone wants to demagogue everyone else. That may be good politics, but it's awful policy.

Sometimes, when you see the newspaper and you read something I said, you say, 'Oh, I can't believe he said that.'

I think America needs lots of tough people. Not just me. I think America needs to get tougher, all of us.

The people elected us to end the talk and to act decisively.

You're saying 'will it become politically unpopular to have the position I'm having.' If it does, so be it.

The argument for getting our own house in order is not an argument for turning our back on the world. We cannot and should not do that.

I can guarantee you this, that more pension and benefit reforms which I will consider arbitration reform to be one of them, are things that when they come to my desk, they will be signed.

The people of New Jersey stepped up. They shared in the sacrifice. You know what else they did? They rewarded politicians who lead instead of politicians who pandered.

Today is the day for the complaining to end and for statesmanship to begin. Today I am taking action to cut state spending and balance the budget this year.

You just have to stand and grit your teeth and know your poll numbers are going to go down - and mine have - but you gotta grit through it because the alternative is unacceptable.

Now our founding fathers had the wisdom to know that social acceptance and popularity were fleeing, and that this country's principles needed to be rooted in strengths greater than the passions and the emotions of the times.

Now, in New Jersey, we have more government workers per square mile than any state in America. But since I've been governor we now have fewer people on the state payroll at any time since Christie Whitman left office in January 2001. That's the right direction, Mr. President, not the wrong direction.

I am not going to make any commitments to the teachers union to do anything until they do something that's other than in their own self- interest. And everything they have done so far is in their self-interests, and that's it.

It's not that I'm universally loved. We know I'm not in New Jersey. But what they do say in New Jersey is, 'We like him, and we think he's telling us the truth.' I think we need to have that type of politics on the national level.

Now, do I think there has to be shared sacrifice among other nations in the world who want a stable and secure world? Absolutely, there has to be. But I don't think that America can ever abdicate its leadership role in the world because of who we are and where we've come from. We are the symbol for the world for freedom and liberty.

And I think if the president's made a mistake here, it's this laid-back kind of approach where he's waiting for someone else to solve the problem. Some people say it's a political strategy. No matter what it is, it's not effective in solving problems.

I don't think there's anybody in America who thinks my personality is best suited to being Number Two.

I am pro-life, I believe in exceptions for rape, incest and the life of the mother. That's my position, take it or leave it.

And on this you have my pledge - unlike in the past, when you stood up and did what was right, this governor will not pull the rug out from underneath you - I will sign strong reform bills.

Is there any wonder why we are in such big trouble? Any question why the people don't trust their government anymore, and demand a change?

I believe marriage should be between one man and one woman. That's my view, and that'll be the view of our state because I wouldn't sign a bill that - like the one that was in New York.

Now, we believe that the majority of teachers in America know our system must be reformed, to put students first so that

America can compete, that teachers don't teach to become rich or famous. They teach because they love children.

Ted Cruz

We need to remain a nation that doesn't just welcome but that celebrates legal immigrants who come here seeking to pursue the American Dream.

I would do anything and I will continue to do anything I can to stop the train wreck that is Obamacare.

I think it's an enormous blessing to be the child of an immigrant who fled oppression, because you realize how fragile liberty is and how easily it can be taken away.

It took Jimmy Carter to give us Ronald Reagan.

This election presents a stark choice - we can continue down the road of the Obama Democrats, more and more spending, debt and government control of the economy, or we can return to the founding principles of our nation - free markets, fiscal responsibility and individual liberty.

A friend of mine, a Hispanic entrepreneur asked me a question sometime ago, he said, 'When is the last time you saw a Hispanic panhandler?' I think it's a great question. I'll tell you, in my life I've never once have seen a Hispanic panhandler, because in our community, it would be viewed as shameful to be out on the street begging.

We are seeing a great awakening. A national movement of We the People, brought together by what unites us - a shared love of liberty, and an understanding of the unlimited potential of free men and free women.

One of biggest lies in politics is the lie that Republicans are the party of big business. Big business does great with big government. Big business is very happy to climb in bed with big government.

Republicans are and should be the party of small business and of entrepreneurs.

When my father came over here penniless with $100 sewn into his underwear, thank God some well-meaning liberal didn't come put his arm around him and say, 'Let me take care of you.'

I think Hispanic community - the values that resonate in our community are fundamentally conservative. They are faith, family and patriotism. Do you know the rate of military enlistment among Hispanics is higher than any demographic in this country? And they are also hard work and responsibility.

I've really had two heroes in my life. My father and Ronald Reagan.

Look, I think Hispanic community - the values that resonate in our community are fundamentally conservative. They are faith, family and patriotism.

The American free market system is the greatest engine for prosperity and opportunity that the world has ever seen. Freedom works.

The most enduring legacy of President Barack Obama is going to be a new generation of leaders standing up for liberty.

Millions of Americans are standing up and saying, 'We want our country back!' Republicans, Democrats, Independents, will not go down the path of Greece, we will not go quietly into the night.

Christians are being systematically exterminated.

What I have been talking about for many years is opportunity conservatism, that every policy should focus like a laser on easing the means of ascent up the economic ladder.

We are here today because of grass-roots conservatives all over the place. That's the way the democratic process is supposed to work. It's not supposed to be a bunch of guys in a smoky room in Austin picking the next Senator.

How do we turn our nation around? President Obama thinks the answer is more and more government. Government is not the answer. You are not doing anyone a favor by creating dependency, destroying individual responsibility.

It's tragic from how far we've come from 'Hope and Change'.

The strength of our economy allows us to maintain the mightiest military in the world, effectively enforcing a Pax Americana.

Every day, I come home with a spring in my step. We've got to work together to stop the Obama agenda and take this country back.

If you support amnesty, you should vote for the Democrats.

Hispanic unemployment is higher than the national average and when the federal government is killing small businesses and killing jobs it is hurting the future of the Hispanic community and we need to carry that message.

I am perfectly happy to compromise and work with anybody: Republicans, Democrats, Libertarians - I'll work with Martians if - and the if is critical - they're willing to cut spending and reduce the debt.

The people who suffer in the Obama economy have been young people, African Americans, Hispanics, single moms.

The reason why I'm a conservative is because conservative policies work and they improve opportunities. They are the avenue for climbing the economic dream.

Every American, I think, should be able to fill out their taxes on a postcard.

Stopping bad things is a significant public service.

What I try to keep an eye on is I don't work for the party bosses in Washington. I work for 26 million Texans.

Going to school on a campus where the faculty overwhelmingly disagrees with you, and where the student body overwhelmingly disagrees with you, is challenging. If you go in without a firm foundation, it can undermine what you believe.

I'm a lot less concerned with Bill Clinton's escapades decades ago than I am with

Hillary Clinton's consistently wrong record when it comes to foreign policy, when it comes to domestic policy.

Voters are hungry for principled, conservative fighters - because the threat to our liberties from Washington never has been greater.

The essence of the conservative message should be we want a dynamic nation where anybody with nothing can achieve anything.

I don't think it's government's job to find health care for people. I think it's the individual's job to find health care.

We are witnessing a great awakening. Millions of Texans, millions of Americans are rising up to reclaim our country, to defend liberty and to restore the Constitution.

Do you know the rate of military enlistment among Hispanics is higher than any demographic in this country?

Far too many candidates wear their faith on their sleeve.

President Reagan stood for conservative principles in a way that brought people together.

My mother was born in Wilmington, Delaware. She's a U.S. citizen, so I'm a U.S. citizen.

Christians have no greater ally than Israel.

Cloture is simply cutting off debate.

If you hate the Jewish people, you are not reflecting the teachings of Christ.

If you will not stand with Israel and the Jews, then I will not stand with you.

It is the job of our military to protect America and to hunt down and kill those who would threaten to murder Americans.

On issue after issue, the Obama Administration has openly ignored, defied, and unilaterally tried to change the law.

On issue after issue, the Obama Administration has openly ignored, defied, and unilaterally tried to change the law.

The Second Amendment is an integral part of the Bill of Rights.

What Obamacare does is decreases choices and drives up cost.

When you subpoena one pastor, you subpoena every pastor.

If you think back to the fight over drones, when I was proud to be standing shoulder to shoulder with Rand Paul filibustering for 13 hours, that was viewed as a fringe issue, as a quixotic issue, and yet millions of Americans engaged, spoke up, got online.

There is overwhelming bipartisan support outside of Washington that we need to finally secure our borders, enforce our laws, and stop the problem of illegal immigration.

We need to conceptualize; we need to articulate conservative domestic policy with a laser focus on opportunity, on easing the means of ascent up the economic ladder.

Is it true that the American people are war-weary? Absolutely. We are tired of sending our sons and daughters to distant lands year after year after year, to give their lives trying to transform foreign nations.

It's critical to have a sound foundation in free-market economics and the Constitution. A great many Republicans in Washington don't have that foundation.

My dad came from Cuba when he was a teenager not speaking English. And I grew up here speaking Spanglish. That's the world in which I grew up, and that's a world in which a lot of second generation immigrants find themselves.

One of the specific powers and responsibilities of the federal government is to secure the borders. Property can be taken with due process of law and just compensation.

Having principled men and women in office is how you protect yourself from tyranny, and that was something I learned from when I was 2, 3, 5 years old.

I don't think the federal government has any business keeping a list of law-abiding Americans who exercise their constitutional right to keep and bear arms.

I introduced legislation in the Senate to prohibit President Obama's amnesty. The House of Representatives stood up and led. It took the legislation I introduced and it passed it. But the Senate Democrats stood as one uniform block and said, 'No, we will do nothing to stop amnesty.'

I'm always amused when the 'New York Times' writes editorials trying to be helpful to Republicans and say, 'This is the way Republicans can save themselves.' Look, the 'New York Times' disagrees with us. They're entitled to disagree with us, but it's not like we should take their advice.

On the Left, the best and brightest go into politics - Barack Obama is the epitome of the perfect leftist. On the Right, the best and brightest go make money. Very few conservatives want to endure all the nonsense you have to put up with to run for office.

The single best thing we can do is expand competition. Let people purchase health insurance across state lines. If you want to expand access, what you want to do is increase choices and drive down cost.

The Washington establishment think Republicans win elections by you don't stand for anything, you keep your head down, you don't rock the boat. You know what? Every time we do that, we get clobbered in the polls.

There is a problem in Washington, and the problem is bigger than a continuing resolution. It is bigger than Obamacare. It is even bigger than the budget. The most fundamental problem and the frustration is that the men and women in Washington aren't listening.

There is no more an enthusiastic advocate of legal immigration in the U.S. Senate than

I am, and that is a message that resonates powerfully in the Hispanic community.

There's an old joke that politics is Hollywood for ugly people. An awful lot of the press coverage about Washington reads like coverage of Hollywood. Madonna is having some spat with Sean Penn. Who cares? And who cares which politician is mad at that politician?

When Mitt Romney talked about Putin expanding his sphere of influence, Obama mocked and said, 'The Cold War has been over 20 years, nothing to be worried about'... We keep making that mistake with Putin.

You always have to be worried about something that is considered a so-called 'scientific theory' that fits every scenario. Climate change, as they've defined it, can never be disproved.

I do not believe any president can bind a successor president to give up his fundamental role as protector of the country.

I'm not cool enough to hang out with any rock stars. Jay-Z doesn't come over to my house. I don't hang out with Ted Nugent.

It's not the job of the U.S. military to do nation-building or produce democratic utopias.

Often you see big companies, big banks who are eager to embrace crushing regulatory burdens because they drive up everyone's costs.

The American president has a peculiar leadership responsibility to speak out for freedom.

The authority to declare war rests in Congress, not in an out-of-control president.

The single biggest surprise about arriving to the Senate is the defeatist attitude here.

The United States has a responsibility to defend our values.

You'd better believe that Putin sees that in Syria, Obama draws a red line and ignores the red line.

After 2012, all of the Washington political consultants and all the mainstream media came to Republicans and said, 'You've got to do better with Hispanics, and the way to do better with Hispanics is to embrace amnesty.' And, look, a lot of Republicans in Washington were scared.

I am far more a fan of aggressive entrepreneurs than I am of major CEOs. You look at major CEOs, and they are almost to a person quite timid. They don't act to defend the free market principles that are vital to growth.

I suspect I was not the first 21-year-old who thought he knew more than he did. And one of the virtues of age, one of the virtues of getting married and becoming a father, is it often leads one to take a more measured approach to life.

It has been suggested that those of us who are fighting to defend liberty - fighting to turn around the out-of-control spending and out-of-control debt in this country, fighting to defend the Constitution, it has been suggested that we are wacko birds.

It's remarkable that the failures of the Obama, Clinton, Kerry foreign policy are not only uniting the Left and Right in Israel but might even be creating some common ground between Israel and the Palestinian Authority.

Millions of people are asking for accountability, for responsibility, for truth from their elected officials, truth about how

Obamacare is failing the men and women of America.

Unfortunately, the Senate Democrats have become an extreme party. They have become a party that has abdicated their responsibilities. Under Harry Reid and the Senate Democrats, we have a do-nothing Senate.

Carly Fiorina

My mother taught me about the power of inspiration and courage, and she did it with a strength and a passion that I wish could be bottled.

The truth is, I'm proud of the life I've lived so far, and though I've made my share of mistakes, I have no regrets.

When you challenge other people's ideas of who or how you should be, they may try to diminish and disgrace you. It can happen in small ways in hidden places, or in big ways on a world stage. You can spend a lifetime resenting the tests, angry about the slights and the injustices. Or, you can rise above it.

Once I dive in, I dive in all the way.

This world is clearly emerging before our eyes. The shifts ahead, the opportunities ahead are massive.

I love being a woman. I like dressing up; I love buying shoes.

Leadership comes in small acts as well as bold strokes.

You have to master not only the art of listening to your head, you must also master listening to your heart and listening to your gut.

People's ideas and fears can make them small but they cannot make you small. People's prejudices can diminish them but they cannot diminish you. Small-minded people can think they determine your worth. But only you can determine your worth.

 If a decision-making process is flawed and dysfunctional, decisions will go awry.

The truth is in California you can't build a new manufacturing facility, and businesses are leaving in droves because of bad government policy.

Do not be afraid to make decisions, do not be afraid to make mistakes.

People who don't fit the mold are treated differently than those who do.

Look, I'm a cancer survivor, all right? So I have great personal empathy for people who have pre-existing conditions and can't get insurance.

If someone believes they are limited by their gender, race or background, they will become more limited.

When you lead change, sometimes you get arrows in your back. I mean, that's just the way the real world is.

I don't give up on commitments until what I've been asked to do is clearly finished.

We need more transparency and accountability in government so that people know how their money is being spent. That means putting budgets online, putting legislation online.

Of course people think Washington is arrogant. It is.

I think somehow men understand other men's need for respect differently than they understand it for a woman. I'm disappointed to have to say that, but I think it's undeniably true.

A leader's most important decisions are about people. Who do you put in which jobs? How long do you leave them in a job?

You know, Californians care about protecting their environment. So do I. But they also care about that in the context of a healthy economy.

You know, I believe that marriage is between a man and a woman.

I started out as a receptionist. I typed, I filed, I answered the phones for a little nine-person company.

A woman's experience is different from a man's in virtually every respect, including how she is treated by the media.

Fiscal policy is not just, or even not even principally, the purview of the president.

I think bolstering free trade is a boon to the dollar.

I'm not a professional politician, I'm a problem solver.

I think we ought to ban earmarks. I think we ought to give citizens the opportunity to designate up to 10 percent of their federal income tax toward debt reduction. If we did that, we would reduce our debt by $95 billion a year.

Many people see technology as the problem behind the so-called digital divide. Others see it as the solution. Technology is neither. It must operate in conjunction with business, economic, political and social system.

You do not need to have a 2,400-page bill come out of Washington, D.C.

You don't create jobs by passing bills, you create jobs by cutting taxes.

I felt disconnected from the decisions made in Washington and, to be honest, really didn't think my vote mattered because I didn't have a direct line of sight from my vote to a result.

You know, I believe that technology is the great leveler. Technology permits anybody to play. And in some ways, I think technology - it's not only a great tool for democratization, but it's a great tool for eliminating prejudice and advancing meritocracies.

When our most important issue is the debt that we're piling on our children and grandchildren, I think it's pretty helpful to have someone in the U.S. Senate who has actually managed billions of dollars and knows how to cut billions of dollars.

Well, I've been a Republican for all of my voting life.

I don't take on a fight just for a fight. I don't tilt at windmills.

I know why jobs go, and I know why they come.

I lost my job in the most public way possible, and the press had a field day with it all over the world. And guess what? I'm still here.

Don't think of yourself as a woman in business.

I am a conservative and proud of it.

I certainly support civil unions.

I really believe that all CEO pay should be voted on by shareholders ahead of time. Mine was.

I think a strong dollar is the result of policies, but I don't think the strong dollar is in and of itself a policy.

I think when you've been a career politician for 34 years you have to run on your record.

I've never thought in terms of 'men do this' and 'women do that.'

It's the federal government's job to secure the border.

People have decided that career politicians may be part of the problem, not part of the solution.

People have decided that career politicians may be part of the problem, not part of the solution.

Any work that's worth doing has its challenges as well as its opportunities. That's true if you're running a business, it's true if you're trying to help on a campaign.

But ours was intended to be a citizen government. It is what of, by and for the people means. And when our most important issue in California is the creation of jobs, I think it's quite helpful to have someone in the U.S. Senate or in the governor's seat who actually knows where jobs come from.

I think it would help tremendously to have a senator that knows where jobs come from, that knows how to create them, that knows how to bring them back and, importantly, knows what it means to manage billions of dollars' worth of expenses and cut billions of dollars' worth of expenses.

If you have a line of business - I know this as a CEO - or if you have a teenager - I know this as a parent - who have a spending problem, what do you do? You quit giving them money.

The GAO just released a report that said 22 percent of federal programs fail to meet their objectives. The truth is we don't know how taxpayer money is spent in Washington, D.C., which is why I think we ought to put every agency budget up on the Internet for everyone to see.

Trey Gowdy

The reason I like the criminal justice system is there aren't Republican or Democrat victims or police officers or prosecutors. It's about respect for the rule of law!

There's a reason that students don't grade their own papers. There's a reason defendants don't sentence themselves. And there's the reason the State Department doesn't get to investigate itself, determine whether or not it made errors in Benghazi. That is Congress's job.

Facts are neither Republican nor Democrat.

If you can turn off certain categories of law, do you not also have the power to turn off all categories of law?

If you were summoned for jury duty and you didn't show up, what would happen? You'd be in jail!

You may be less likely to pick on someone if you don't know what's in their briefcase or purse.

I don't have an issue with whether - from a legal standpoint, with whether or not government can impose the ultimate punishment on people. We do it in capital cases. Police officers shoot fleeing felons.

October of 2011, Occupy protestors descended upon McPherson Square, and they decided to stay. Despite the clear language of the law, these protestors camped at McPherson Square with the definition of camping being sleeping or preparing to sleep.

The longer you remain silent, the longer you don't turn over documents, a presumption begins to build that you're withholding something. That's human nature. That may not be a legal presumption, but that's a common sense presumption.

When you go into public service, you understand you're trading something. You want to feel good about what you do, but you're not going to make what people in private sector make.

I thought that was the crown jewel of the reporter's resume - to actually go to jail protecting a source.

When people in positions of trust mislead us - either recklessly, negligently or intentionally - that impacts the republic.

Benghazi matters because Americans deserve to know the truth from those entrusted to lead and govern.

For 16 years I spoke in trial metaphors, and perhaps I need to get out of that habit.

I believe being a good senator requires two things. Number one, acumen. Number two, interest.

I do not want to stay in Washington.

I was on the campaign trail for 18 months. I never got a question about the District of Columbia in South Carolina.

It always matters whether or not you can trust your government.

The notion that the First Amendment has no limitations whatsoever is balderdash.

The United States attorney in South Carolina was a Barack Obama appointee. Politically, he is to the left of Mao Zedong.

There's no use to having the majority if you are going to be hamstrung by your perception of political vicissitudes.

You don't get John Gotti to testify against his driver. You get the driver to testify against John Gotti.

Even someone as lowly as an assistant U.S. attorney has to undergo a background check, and you're asked a series of very invasive questions, and you're expected to tell the truth and they're under penalty of perjury. And you're asked those questions so you can't be blackmailed or extorted.

It is actually costlier to hire an immigrant. And yet the farm worker is almost invariably an immigrant.

I suspect that with men like General Petraeus, where honor means something - losing your life is secondary to losing your honor.

Honestly, I have heard a lot in my 16 years as a prosecutor.
I cannot and will not raise money on Benghazi. I also advise my colleagues to follow suit.

I don't like bonuses for public services employees who do great jobs, like prosecutors or judges.

I listen to Gov. Romney have to apologize because he has been successful.

I'm not searching for ways to tell the District of Columbia what to do.

I'm unelectable in the District of Columbia.

There's several different forms of executive privilege. The one that is most absolute would be close advisers talking to the president himself.

Unless your name is Jack Bauer, you cannot make people talk.

I don't think the president had anything to do with Fast and Furious. I'm not sure Eric Holder did, which leads to a conversation about whether he should have known about it.

Nikki Haley

 This is America. Anyone is free to protest about anything they want.

Contraception doesn't define a woman.

I wear heels. It's not for a fashion statement, it's... ammunition.

Everyone can have a bad day.

Ann Romney makes all women proud by the way she has conducted her life as a strong woman of faith, as a mother, as a wife and as a true patriot.

I think that we are at a point in our country where we're trying to decide what role should religion play in the political arena.

I'm not going to stop beating up on the Democrats for wasteful spending.

There is no war on women. Women are doing well. But women are thoughtful. And what we in the Republican Party and across the country, Republican, Independents and Democrat women say is we're more thoughtful than a label. We care about jobs and the economy and healthcare and education. We care about a lot of different things.

Unfortunately, these past few years, you can work hard, try to be as successful as possible, follow the rules, and President Barack Obama will do everything he can to stand in your way.

I don't think we should focus on what church that person walks into .. I think we need to focus on what they do when they walk out of church.

We don't have unions in South Carolina because we don't need unions in South Carolina.

I'm veYou don't go to the people that are just like you. You go to the people that you have to earn their credit.

Protests are fine. But in South Carolina we believe in the rule of law, and the people of this state should never doubt that as governor, I will enforce it.

American businesses deserve a federal government that doesn't stand in their way, not one that tries to chase them overseas.

I'm a huge fan of women; I think we're great.

I'm not going to stop beating up on the unions.

ry proud of the way that I was raised, I'm very proud of the way that my parents raised me.

The public likes to think that women only care about contraception.

I encourage people to find and use the power of their voices just as much when I do not agree with those voices as when I do agree with them.

I had a white senator call me a rag head, and I had an African-American legislator call me a conservative with a tan.

My job is to create jobs. In the end I'm going to have jobs to show for it.

As I said, my parents loved that when they came to America, if you worked hard, the only things that could stop you were the limits you placed on yourself.

In 2009, South Carolina was blessed to welcome a great American company that chose to stay in our country to continue to do business. That company was Boeing.

Almost forty-five years after my parents first became Americans, I stand before you and them tonight as the proud governor of the state of South Carolina.

For a bill to become law, it truly has to be the will of the people, and for a president to stop the will of the people and stop what you're trying to do in your state is not the role of Washington.

I think any label is bad.

People ask the question, 'If you're offered VP, would you take it?' No, I won't take it.

All of my policy is not based on a label. It's based on what I lived and what I know.

I think any label is bad. I'm more than a label.

I think the media's a little frightened of women.

Boeing started a new line for their 787 Dreamliner, creating 1,000 new jobs in South Carolina, giving our state a shot in the arm when we truly needed it.

I've never been a planner. I didn't know I was going to run for the State House. I didn't know I was going to run for governor. I don't know what's next, and I love not thinking about it because the doors open at a certain time.

My parents started a business out of the living room of our home and, 30-plus years later, it was a multimillion dollar company. So, President Obama, with all due respect, don't tell me that my parents didn't build their business.

South Carolinians are strong, independently minded people. At the end of the day, they make their own decisions. And I respect them for that. And I welcome that. And I told him that from the very beginning.

The people of South Carolina support conservatives who are trying to push real change, and the people of South Carolina expect their presidential candidates to back them up when they show courage.

Mike Huckabee

The most important thing about global warming is this. Whether humans are responsible for the bulk of climate change is going to be left to the scientists, but it's all of our responsibility to leave this planet in better shape for the future generations than we found it.

It's when ordinary people rise above the expectations and seize the opportunity that milestones truly are reached.

If the Democrats want to insult women by making them believe that they are helpless without Uncle Sugar coming in and providing for them a prescription each month for birth control because they cannot control their libido or their reproductive system without the help of the government, then so be it.

A leader is the one who can outline the broad vision and the direction, and say here's where we are going to go, here's why we need to go there, and here's how we are going to get there. A manager is the one who actually gets up under the hood and tunes the carburetor.

The health care system is really designed to reward you for being unhealthy. If you are a healthy person and work hard to be healthy, there are no benefits.

Fear is a very explosive emotion, but it has a short life span. It's the sprint. The marathon is hope.

Inside every human being there are treasures to unlock.

Prayer reminds me it's not just about me. It's about all the people with whom I share this planet, and all of whom God has created, and all of whom he cares just as much about as he cares about me.

Pray a little more, work a little harder, save, wait, be patient and, most of all, live within our means. That's the American way. It's not spending ourselves into prosperity or taxing ourselves into prosperity.

Prayer's important, not just as some kind of a metaphysical exercise, but I think it's a way to refresh one's own mind and motive. If you're praying, you're really looking beyond your own personal thoughts and the pressures that are around you.

I wish we would all remember that being American is not just about the freedom we have; it is about those who gave it to us.

I think at the heart of the pro-life movement is the idea that all people are created equal, endowed by their creator with certain unalienable rights starting with life.

We ask why there is violence in our schools, but we have systematically removed God from our schools.

One thing governors feel, Democrats and Republicans alike, is that we have a health care system that, if you're on Medicaid, you have unlimited access to health care, at unlimited levels, at no cost. No wonder it's running away.

Divorce is one of the key predictors of poverty for a child growing up in a home that's broken.

I've said that, that I've felt like as Christians and particularly even as Republicans, we needed to address issues that touched the broader perspective, and that included disease, hunger, poverty, homelessness, the environment.

I think people forget that bipartisanship is really the burden of the victor, not the loser.

I have a little pocket Bible that I have with me all the time in my briefcase, and so usually in the mornings, sometimes on the campaign bus or plane, I always try to catch some time to do that regularly.

I was a timid little guy when I was a kid. I used humor as a defense; I became the class clown. But deep inside, I felt real vulnerable.

I've twice run against women opponents, and it's a very different kind of approach. For those of us who have some chivalry left, there's a level of respect... You treat some things as a special treasure; you treat other things as common.

Jesus said, 'Blessed are the peacemakers.' And I think a lot of people don't understand that there's a difference between a peace lover and a peacemaker. Everybody loves peace, but wearing jewelry around your neck and saying 'I love peace' doesn't bring it.

Most single moms are very poor, uneducated, can't get a job, and if it weren't for government assistance, their kids would be starving to death and never have health care. And that's the story that we're not seeing, and it's unfortunate that we glorify and glamorize the idea of out of children wedlock.

Doesn't matter whether it's a teen girl who's pregnant, hasn't told her parents, or an elderly couple dealing with one of them being diagnosed with Alzheimer's. Those are real people to me. Those are the people I dealt with every single day.

Christian conservatives care about their families eating. They're concerned about energy independence. They're concerned about functional government.

I've always suggested if you can't stand the sight of your own blood, don't run for office.

I support workplace clean air. But a federal ban on smoking would mean that you couldn't smoke in your own home. I don't care what people do in their home.

I continue to do something I've done since I was 18, and that is read a chapter of Proverbs every day as part of my daily devotion. I still maintain that.

I think that whether someone is a Christian or not, the idea that a human life has dignity and intrinsic worth should be clear enough.

I would describe myself as a 'total conservative, a conscientious one.'

I'm one of the strongest advocates for the arts you'll ever find!

The fact is, my friends, most Americans don't want more government. They want less government.

Women I know are smart, educated, intelligent, capable of doing anything that anybody else can do.

Your vote can't be separated from your faith.

So when we're really addressing issues like poverty, you can't do that without addressing the real driver of some of those, which is stable homes, families. So that's why to me those issues are important. They're not frivolous. They're critical economic issues.

A political race today, even a primary, is $150 million. The whole political system has become obscene in terms of the absurd amount of money that is required to compete. Just put it on ESPN and call it a sporting event.

Regardless of Bill Clinton's politics or personal life, he grew up in obscurity and was elected to the presidency - twice. Don't take that away from him, because then you take it away from every other kid in America sitting out there in a school bus with a big dream.

As a governor, I've signed virtually every kind of pro-life legislation that we can sign under existing federal law, none of which have been harsh or punitive, but I think they've been important to really point out a pro-life culture in Arkansas. That's, for me, a good thing.

For Democrats to reduce women to beggars for cheap government-funded birth control is demeaning to the women that I know who are far more complicated than their libido and the management of their reproductive system.

I find it unnecessary, useless and frankly a bit unnecessary to get into all sorts of debates over President Obama's religion or the authenticity of his birth. I know for some people that it is an obsession. It is not with me.

I think a lot of people in America do not understand that the basis of true liberty can't happen without an objective moral standard by which we live our lives.

I'm not against anybody. I'm really not. I'm not a hater. I'm not homophobic. I honestly don't care what people do personally in their individual lives.

The United States of America was originally an experiment. But it was an experiment in recognizing God-given individual liberty and creating a government in which we no one is deemed better than another. And in which all of us are equal. Not equal in abilities, but equal in intrinsic worth and value.

There are three basic prerequisites that almost guarantee... that a child won't have a day of poverty. If a person gets married and remains married in a monogamous relationship for life, finishes high school, gets a job, and keeps a job for at least five years, there's a 91 percent likelihood that a... child in that family will not have poverty.

There is an increasing push to compartmentalize faith separately from our life in the public square - and it's not possible - at least, it's not possible if we continue the American tradition of true individual freedom, which also implies individual responsibility. Without an objective moral standard, that's not possible.

How could I get up there and say, 'People, we've got to do better,' when I was the poster child for everything that was wrong? I've always believed leaders don't ask others to do what they're unwilling to do.

Politics has become unbelievably and unfortunately way too much about how much money is involved rather than what kind of ideas are involved.

Marriage has historically, as long as there's been human history, meant a man and a woman in a relationship for life. Once we change that definition, then where does it go from there?

Marriage should be reinforced, not redefined.

The Bible, however, was not created to be amended and altered with each passing culture.

I say Republicans aren't right all the time. Democrats aren't wrong all the time - now, maybe most of the time, but not all the time.

I'm a strong advocate for music. I think guitars are wonderful.

I've never, ever tasted beer.

The biggest gap there is in America is not economic; the gap is spiritual and cultural.

To me, there are four F's in a good tax system: it ought to be flatter, fairer, finite and family-friendly.

Families out there know that if they get in trouble and they've spent up a bunch of money and they've borrowed and they are up to hock to their necks, the thing they've got to do is start paying off what they owe and cut back their spending.

For me, running for office is never about trying to destroy an opponent, be it Democratic or Republican. It really ought to be about how can we solve some problems that we're facing.

Well, for me the pro-life issue has been something I've been very passionate about since the '70s, and I have been very involved in the pro-life community since long before politics.

Government shouldn't try to dictate what art looks like or what it portrays. Last thing we want is government screwing it up, which is what they would do.

I do believe God has given me an incredible opportunity and a platform in a secular environment but still to take a stand for Christ and being a blessing to believers.

I grew up in a family in which no male upstream from me had ever finished high school, much less gone to college. But I was taught that even though there was nothing I could do about what was behind me, I could change everything about what was in front of me. My working poor parents told me that I could do better.

I have often been characterized by one sound bite, and people say, 'That is the whole of Mike Huckabee, because we have him on this off-the-cuff moment.'

I'm always flattered when people on the far Left manufacture a new version of being 'offended.' They can be quite creative in finding something that hurts their feelings.

I'm an independent conservative. And what I mean by that - when I think we're right, I'm with us all the way, and I am a conservative. And I think my record reflects that.

I'm not against gifts that entertain, but I really believe that some of the most valuable gifts that we can give are the things that help us to develop a skill and be entertaining.

I'm not against gifts that entertain, but I really believe that some of the most valuable gifts that we can give are the things that help us to develop a skill and be entertaining.

Things that have happened with Enron and companies like that, where they've squandered their employees' pension funds, I think it has brought a new level of anxiety. People don't feel like they can trust their employer.

Darrel Issa

You can call me a pain. I'll accept that as a compliment.

It's very simple. If the American people care about a lot of things including corruption in government, then, in fact, if you use the power to appoint in order to do political business, to clear fields, to save your party money and so on, if it's not a crime - and I believe it is - it certainly is business as usual, politics of corruption.

The debate on how to shrink the federal government is at the core of our problem of government not doing its job.

Cleveland's a great place when you're a kid. You hardly ever get sunburned, without the sun shining.

The American people have a right to except that the rule of law will guarantee that even if we don't like the policy, that it's done properly.

I've always been fond of the saying that when it comes to oversight and reform, the federal government does two things well: nothing and overreact.

Some people want to amass a great amount of wealth and make a great looking obituary. I'm going to die with more money than is good to leave my son.

Well, I'm going to try to make a real difference in Washington's spending patterns.

I don't need to be looking at every failure of government, I need to be looking where failure of government needs reform.

Every ISP is being attacked, maliciously both from in the United States and outside of the United States, by those who want to invade people's privacy. But more importantly they want to take control of computers, they want to hack them, they want to steal information.

Every portal coming into this country is being attacked by those who would harvest information, both national security secrets and just the common information of private individuals and private individuals. That crime is going on, every day, on a single entity known as the Internet.

Remember, America's greatness is based on creating wealth like the rest of the world has never known, and then, making sure it's shared throughout a middle class and even the underprivileged.

Too often, a problem is allowed to fester until it reaches a crisis point... and the American people are left asking the question: what went wrong and why?

My father and all my uncles on both sides served in the military in World War II and Korea.

Some people say that watching pay freezes in the government is like watching water freeze. It expands.

The American people do not want ambassadorships or any other position handed out to save a party money.

You want to toe the line with tough investigations without falling into political grandstanding inherent in Washington on both sides of the aisle.

Bureaucracies tend to grow and to brag about their growth based on how many individuals they have and how much money they spend.

Everyone has a past.

I was brought up in a household with sir and ma'am.

If there was a blog with five listeners or viewers, I had to be on it. Now I have to be on fewer media, but more substantive media.

In America, we're trying to find a peaceful solution in the Middle East and we're not going to be divided along any lines, including religious lines, including ethnic backgrounds.

The American people have a right to know on the rare occasions in which their money is used to invest in private operations, if you will, take bets on capitalism, that is very well vetted, very well thought out and without political interference.

You know, it doesn't take a genius in the private sector to know that you can save literally hundreds of billions of dollars in federal spending if you can make it more responsive. That's the main job.

Bobby Jindal

It's time to update traditional public schools, charter schools, home schools, online schools and parochial schools. Let the dollars follow the child instead of forcing the child to follow the dollars, so that every child has the opportunity to attain an education.

We should increase our development of alternative fuels, taking advantage of renewable resources, like using corn and sugar to produce ethanol or soybeans to produce biodiesel.

We need an equal opportunity society, one in which government does not see its job as picking winners and losers. Where do you go if you want special favors? Government. Where do you go if you want a tax break? Government. Where do you go if you want a handout? Government. This must stop.

The recent riots in France demonstrate the problem European countries face where second and third generation immigrants still do not consider themselves French, German, or English.

On Thanksgiving I will stop to give thanks that my family is safe and healthy, especially because I realize that, following the tragedies of this year, it is all too real a possibility that they might not have been.

The politically correct crowd is tolerant of all viewpoints, except those they disagree with.

The Obama presidency, and liberalism in general, are based on not trusting the American people - a belief that big government is better for people.

Police officials routinely execute search warrants on private homes and offices, and Congressional offices should not be treated any differently. There cannot be one set of rules for elected officials and another set of rules for everyone else.

Our culture, language, history, and values are vital to uniting us as a nation.

The Republican party does have a lot of work to do. But changing our principles is not a winning strategy. We need to modernize, not moderate.

Here's what I've found in Louisiana: The voters want to know what you believe, what you stand for, and what you plan to do, not what shade your skin is.

I remember when TV networks believed in the First Amendment. It is a messed up situation when Miley Cyrus gets a laugh, and Phil Robertson gets suspended.

The Nation needs to take a new approach to our energy problems.

Anybody who spends time off of Louisiana's shores can recognize that these oysters are not endangered. To classify them as such risks great harm to not only fishermen who make their living collecting oysters in the Gulf, but also to Louisiana's economy in total.

When a law enforcement officer apprehends an illegal immigrant, it makes no sense to simply release that individual who has been breaking our laws with no threat of sanction or penalty.

Finally, we should help developing nations like China and India curb their exponentially increasing consumption of oil and natural gas, which is driving world prices higher.

As we embrace the American dream and the freedoms it represents, we must also ensure that those who wish to enjoy those freedoms become a part of our society and learn to speak our language.

You can look at that by comparing Medicare's growth rates to the private insurance world, to the other Federal programs that we run, by looking at the billions of dollars, not millions but billions of dollars, we waste every year.

India, in particular, is looking to develop nuclear power for domestic, commercial use, and we should work with them. This is a good deal for both countries.

Members of Congress must live according to the same laws as everyone else.

Unfortunately, we are finding the bureaucratic inefficiencies and red tape have a tendency to slow the efforts of individuals and communities working to rebuild.

Conservative ideas don't just sound good. They actually work. That's the secret of our success.

In the aftermath of September 11th, it is critical to secure our borders.

As everyone in Louisiana knows, there was often no communication or coordination between the state and federal government in the aftermath of Hurricanes Katrina and Rita.

When I ran for Congress I promised to help make health care affordable again.

First, we must stop issuing drivers' licenses to people in our country illegally. Providing them with forms of government identification makes a mockery of our laws and undermines national security efforts.

The threat of terrorism is great and with today's porous borders, someone could bring a biological weapon into our country or sneak a dirty bomb across unmanned portions of our borders.

We need to break our dependency on foreign sources of oil, which leaves us at the mercy of foreign powers. To do that, we should increase domestic energy production.

Here's an idea: How about just 'Americans?' That has a nice ring to it, if you ask me. Placing undue emphasis on our 'separateness' is a step backward. Bring back the melting pot.

Congress did a good thing back in 1995 in passing the Deep Water Royalty Relief Act. That act did a simple thing. It provided automatic royalty relief for new leases for 5 years in the deep waters of the Gulf of Mexico.

Thirty percent of the Nation's energy comes off the gulf coast.

Mia Love

Difficult things aren't easy, but they're worth it.

The America I know is great - not because government made it great but because ordinary citizens like me, like my father and like you are given the opportunity every day to do extraordinary things.

Regardless of the difficulties we may face individually, in our families, in our communities and in our nation, the old adage is still true - you can make excuses or you can make progress, but you cannot make both! The America I know doesn't make excuses.

I will tell them that you can work hard, you can improve your life and the lives of your children in one day when you deliver your youngest child to the university, you will look her in the eye and say, 'You will give back.'

So the America I came to know growing up was filled with all the excitement and possibilities found in living the American dream.

The government is not your salvation. The government is not your road to prosperity. Hard work, education will take you far beyond what any government program can ever promise.

Growing up, I had a front row seat to seeing two people work really hard. My dad scrubbed toilets at a private Catholic school for a while, and that was to help me get through school.

What are the Democrats, the party of Jim Matheson, telling them? The message of the Democrats is that the Amercian dream is over. 'The government is all you have. Give up your dreams, and the government will save you, the government will heal you, the government will be your hope and change.' We know here in Utah, none of that is true.

President Obama's version of America is a divided one - pitting us against each other based on our income level, gender, and social status. His policies have failed! We are not better off than we were 4 years ago, and no rhetoric, bumper sticker, or campaign ad can change that.

The Democrats have come right out and said it: the power of the central government shall have no limits at all.

I understand people, and I think that my life and my history and what I represent can relate to a lot of the women, the independents, the moderate voters.

According to liberals, I'm not supposed to exist. I know that I am going to be a target for the Left. I have something to say to them: 'Game On.'

The influence I would hope to have is to create an environment where we're not singling Americans out - that we are creating opportunities for all Americans. Not saying, 'I'm going to funnel money into your city so that you're completely dependent on government.'

Barack Obama's class warfare will not work on this Republican nominee. Not in Utah.

This is the America we know because we built it.

I believe this country is in real trouble, and it's up to us, to fix it before its too late.

My parents immigrated to the United States with $10 in their pocket and a belief that the America they had heard about really did exist as the land of opportunity.

John Kasich

Affirmative action has a negative effect on our society when it means counting us like so many beans and dividing us into separate piles.

A great power has to have the discipline not only to go when necessary but to know when not to go. Getting involved in ethnic, religious civil wars is a recipe for disaster.

If we intend to provide a better life, and a better world, for future generations, we can't ignore the quality of the environment we leave them.

When Governor Romney was out here, I told him, I said, 'we are following the formula of streamlining regulations, being job creating friendly, balancing budgets, cutting taxes, and, you know, using common sense. And if you get to be president, we are going to do more of that.'

When we give a subsidy, the benefits to the public ought to exceed the benefits to the company. When it doesn't, that's our definition of corporate welfare.

When I left Washington, we actually had a balanced budget and we paid down the most amount of the national debt in modern history and cut taxes and created jobs. And I was the chief architect of that plan in '97.

We've unveiled the most comprehensive reform budget people have seen in a generation.

And what we're doing in Ohio is we're moving from a basic manufacturing economy to one that's diversified, including energy and health care and agriculture and IT.

And, frankly, what happens out of Washington is, it creates a wind in my face, uncertainty over Obamacare, uncertainty over their tax policy, uncertainty over the regulatory policy.

I want to tell you ladies and gentlemen, the actions that we took were not always easy. The actions that we took were not always popular. But when you get yourself in public office, you must lead, you must do what's necessary.

This is not about Republican or Democrat. It is about our children, it's about our families, it is about our country, and frankly, ladies and gentlemen, it is about the world. We've got to leave here and march, and make sure Mitt Romney and Paul Ryan are president and vice president of the United States.

You know where entrepreneurship in my opinion has to go? Into the inner city.

I think he should let me run Ohio. He should let us, the legislature, the members there, we should be running Ohio. The states are the laboratories out here, and I think the president needs to mind to the problems that he has in Washington.

What people really want to know from their doctor is, are you going to make me feel better? And what they really want to know from a president are, are you going to give me some security when it comes to my work? Because if I'm not working, my family is in trouble. And when I am working, the fact of the matter is, my whole family is doing better.

I mean, the fact of the matter is, Ohio 's coming back because we set a clear path, we cut taxes, we balanced our budget, we got credit upgrades when the whole rest of the world, including America , was being downgraded.

I think we can have some tax reform, but that doesn't mean tax increases. We ought to make the, the rates flatter. We ought to get rid of a bunch of those loopholes.

Ohio's doing what it can do, but I wish they'd get their act together in Washington.

Every time I go to Washington, I break out in a cold sweat. So I try not to spend too much time there.

I'm a believer in bipartisanship.

The reason we have such a reform budget is because we've been thinking about these things for a long time.

And you know what? At the end of the day, it gets down to Obama and Romney. And what it's going to get down to is this. Obama is going to say, 'I inherited a mess and I'm making it better.' And Romney is going to say, 'you haven't made it good enough. And I can do far better than you have done.'

It's not trickle down economics. The problem that the president has is that he's rudderless on the economy. I mean, he doesn't quite know what to do. It's a wake-up on Monday and try to figure it out. It takes time to turn a supertanker, so you need to know where you need to go.

But, at the end of the day, we need to represent the taxpayers who have made enormous sacrifices. Many have lost their jobs. Many of them have seen their companies - they don't have a pension - they have seen their companies cut the match for their 401(k). They have seen their health care benefits be shredded.

Mitt Romney has a history of being a great job creator. Secondly, he was a great governor. He went from billions of dollars in the hole when he became governor to billions of dollars in surplus when he left. And he went from the loss of tens of thousands jobs when he became governor to the creation of 40,000 new jobs when he left office.

So when they don't have certainty, they go the other way. In Ohio, we have given them certainty and things have been improved. But if we can get a Romney presidency, they are going to get much better.

Rand Paul

The history of African-American repression in this country rose from government-sanctioned racism. Jim Crow laws were a product of bigoted state and local governments.

We must always embrace individual liberty and enforce the constitutional rights of all Americans-rich and poor, immigrant and native, black and white.

The Stamp Act was a direct tax imposed on the colonies by King George III. This act inevitably led to the American Revolution. Just as the Stamp Act did in 1765, Obamacare should act as a wake-up call. Chief Justice Roberts provides us with a similar call to action.

What gets lost is that the Republican Party has always been the party of civil rights and voting rights.

What gets lost is that the Republican Party has always been the party of civil rights and voting rights.

Because Republicans believe that the federal government is limited in its function-some have concluded that Republicans are somehow inherently insensitive to minority rights. Nothing could be further from the truth.

I have a message from the Tea Party, a message that is loud and clear and does not mince words. We've come to take our government back.

Just because a couple people on the Supreme Court declare something to be 'constitutional' does not make it so.

If our freedom is taken, the American dream will wither and die.

If you hear me out, I believe you'll discover that what motivates me more than any other issue is the defense of everyone's rights.

I tell people I won't vote to go to war unless I'm ready to go or send my kids.

In our state, I'm really proud of the fact that the ones who overturned Jim Crow in Kentucky were Republicans fighting against an entirely unified Democrat Party. So I am proud to be Republican. I can't imagine being anything else.

A free society will abide unofficial, private discrimination, even when that means allowing hate-filled groups to exclude people based on the color of their skin.

And when the time is right, I hope that African Americans will again look to the party of emancipation, civil liberty, and individual freedom.

You know, when Republicans were in charge, we doubled the debt. But, now, our concern is the Democrats are in charge and they're tripling the debt. So, really, our concern is that we want smaller government.

You campaigned against rich people and you got enough envy whipped up in the country and you're gonna get 'em. You're gonna stick it to those rich people. But guess what? You may not get anymore revenue. You may not get anymore economic growth. But you can say, 'I stuck it to the rich people.'

You campaigned against rich people and you got enough envy whipped up in the country and you're gonna get 'em. You're gonna stick it to those rich people. But guess what? You may not get anymore revenue. You may not get anymore economic growth. But you can say, 'I stuck it to the rich people.'

Of strong importance to me is the defense of minority rights, not just racial minorities, but ideological and religious minorities.

You can't have it both ways. You can't tell me that you're taxed enough already, and that you want constitutional government and then in the next breath say, 'Bring me home some bacon.' The pig has been picked clean.

I have a question, a question for the president: Do you hate all rich people, or just rich people who don't contribute to your campaign? Do you hate poor people or do you just hate poor people with jobs?

Do we fear terrorism so much that we throw out our Constitution, and are we unwilling and afraid to debate our Constitution?

I don't want to live in a nanny state where people are telling me where I can go and what I can do.

Let's means-test benefits - let's means-test Social Security and Medicare and make the rich pay more for these benefits.

You know, you look at term limits, you poll term limits, 70, 80 percent of Republicans or Democrats are for it.

American inventiveness and the desire to build developed because we were guaranteed the right to own our success.

I don't care if you're a Republican or a Democrat, there is something profoundly un-American about using the brute force of government to bully someone.

Washington is horribly broken. We are encountering a day of reckoning and this movement, this Tea Party movement, is a message to Washington that we're unhappy and that we want things done differently.

Foreign aid is not something the vast majority of Americans support, but definitely not conservatives.

Does the owner of the restaurant own his restaurant? Or does the government own his restaurant?

The Republican Party's history is rich and chock full of emancipation and black history.

We should not have drug laws or a court system that disproportionately punishes the black community.

I'm not someone who's sort of still trying to figure out what I believe in.

The Republican promise is for policies that create economic growth. Republicans believe lower taxes, less regulation, balanced budgets, a solvent Social Security and Medicare will stimulate economic growth.

What I've always said is that I'm opposed to institutional racism, and I would've, had I've been alive at the time, I think, had the courage to march with Martin Luther King to overturn institutional racism, and I see no place in our society for institutional racism.

Using taxes to punish the rich, in reality, punishes everyone because we are all interconnected. High taxes and excessive regulation and massive debt are not working.

For most of our history, no one dared to tell Americans, 'you don't build that.'

You shouldn't have one opinion when you're running and another when you're president.

You shouldn't have one opinion when you're running and another when you're president.

All issues of crime are better addressed at the state level.

You don't go into politics unless you want to win.

I think that most manufacturing and mining should be under the purview of state authorities.

What I say is, national defense is the most important thing we do in Washington, but there's still waste in the military budget.

Rick Perry

Crucial to understanding federalism in modern day America is the concept of mobility, or 'the ability to vote with your feet.' If you don't support the death penalty and citizens packing a pistol - don't come to

Texas. If you don't like medicinal marijuana and gay marriage, don't move to California.

There is evil prowling in the world - it shows up in our movies, video games and online fascinations, and finds its way into vulnerable hearts and minds.

Dark economic clouds are dissipating into an emerging blue sky of opportunity.

The God we serve does not seek out the perfect, but instead uses our imperfections and our shortcomings for his greater good. I am humbled by my own limitations. But where I am weak, He is strong.

Guns require a finger to pull the trigger.

The air we breathe, the water we drink, and the land we inhabit are not only critical elements in the quality of life we enjoy - they are a reflection of the majesty of our Creator.

Reforming public education, cutting property taxes, fixing adult and child protective services and funding our budget can all occur when Democrats and Republicans engage in consensus and cooperation - not cynicism and combat.

The liberals think government exists to fix what's wrong with America. They find fault with our Constitution, our economic model and our core values. We disagree with the premise of their argument. We believe there's nothing wrong with America that an extra dose of freedom won't cure.

Our citizens are tired of big government raising their taxes and cooking up new ways to micromanage their lives, our citizens are tired of big government killing jobs with their do-gooder policies. In short the people are Fed Up!

Obamacare has got everyone on edge. I mean, small business - men and women or big business are sitting out there saying we have no idea what this is going to cost, but we know it's going to cost us and cost us a lot.

I am also the product of a place called Paint Creek. Doesn't have a zip code. It's too small to be called a town along the rolling plains of Texas. We grew dryland cotton and wheat, and when I wasn't farming or attending Paint Creek Rural School, I was generally over at Troop 48 working on my Eagle Scout award.

I think Barack Obama is a socialist. I think he cares for his country - don't get me wrong about that - but I think he truly misunderstands what this country was based upon, the values that America was based upon, which was free enterprise and having the ability to risk your capital and having a chance to have a return on your investment.

When a criminal breaks into your home I'll let the liberals call the lawyer. I'm going to call Smith & Wesson.

I want you to answer this question: Why should you settle for anything less than an authentic conservative who will fight for your views and values without an apology? Think about that.

In the myopic world of the liberals, guns are responsible for evil instead of the perpetrator of evil. But criminals are not bound by our laws. That's what makes them criminals.

Armed and law-abiding citizens are a greater deterrent to violent crime than 1,000 laws passed by Congress.

As Americans, we don't see the role of government as guaranteeing outcomes, but allowing free men and women to flourish based on their own vision, their hard work and their personal responsibility.

The fact is there is forgiveness for those who seek God. And I believe in the power of redemption.

It is time to change our policy of appeasement toward the Palestinians, to strengthen our ties with the nation of Israel.

Conservatives are winning offices, and champions of big government are cleaning out their desks right now.

Aggies have a really interesting way of admitting defeat. We've never been outscored. We just ran out of time.

I come by my conservatism authentically, not by convenience. And I offer the American people a new direction.

When I make a vow to God, then I would suggest to you that's even stronger than a handshake in Texas.

It is time to let America be America again. To return freedom to the people. To stand on our founding principles and reject the cynical politics of the Nanny State.

It's time to believe again in the potential of private enterprise set free from the shackles of over-bearing federal government.

I don't think Obama understands basic economics. Not economics that work. He may understand some theory that someone in Princeton sat and dreamed up, but it's not working.

There's places where a secure fence will work, and that strategic type fencing will work. But the idea that people can easily just stand up and say 'let's just build a fence' and be done with it and wipe our hands, and it's going to secure the border, that's not reality.

I grew up in a house with no running water, 16 miles from the closest place that had a post office. I had a very parochial view of the world.

You know, to preserve our job-friendly climate the Texas legislature didn't raise taxes this last legislative session while balancing their budget and maintaining their reserves - and might I add that our budget leaves $6 billion dollars in a rainy day fund?

We do not have to accept our current circumstances. We will change them. We are Americans. That's what we do.

I don't want to look like Connecticut, no offense, I don't want to look like Oklahoma, I don't want to look like California. I want to be uniquely Texas. And that's not to diss anybody else.

We will reverse course on the heavy hand of regulation, discarding Dodd-Frank and any other regulations that advance a political agenda at the expense of jobs and investment on Main Street.

But it wasn't until I graduated from Texas A & M University and joined the United States Air Force, flying C-130's all around the globe, that I truly appreciated the blessings of freedom.

I stand before you today as a disciplined conservative Texan, a committed Republican and a proud American, united with you to restoring our nation and revive the American dream.

To make sure that votes are never canceled out by illegal votes, we instituted a photo ID requirement. And don't you think it's fair to apply at least the same standard required to get a library card or to board an airpane?

My deal is have a flat, simple tax. And - Americans want - Americans I hope - aspire to be - be wealthy. I hope they aspire to have a better quality of life. And we have this class warfare that's going on now. And I don't agree with that. I'm interested in people getting to work.

Washington's insatiable desire to spend our children's inheritance on failed stimulus plans and other misguided economic theories have given record debt and left us with far too many unemployed.

You got to have a courageous president to stand up and says, listen, if - if you send a bill to me that spends more money than what we've coming in, I'll veto it. I mean, I'm going to try to work with you the best I can, but I'm going to veto it.

When it comes to conservative social issues, it saddens me when sometimes my fellow Republicans duck and cover in the face of pressure from the left. Our loudest opponents on the left are never going to like us so let's quit trying to curry favor with them.

Scouting ought to be about building character, not about sex. Period. Precious few parents enroll their boys in the Scouts to get a crash course in sexual orientation.

America's greatness is not found in the size of its government. America's greatness resides in the hearts and the minds of the people.

America needs jobs, smaller government, less spending and a president with the courage to offer more than yet another speech.

If you're looking for a slick politician or a guy with great teleprompter skills, we already have that. He's destroying our economy. I'm a doer, not a talker.

What I learned growing up on the farm was a way of life that was centered on hard work, and on faith and on thrift. Those values have stuck with me my whole life.

Somebody has to tell the E.P.A. that we don't need you monkeying around and fiddling around and getting in our business with every kind of regulation you can dream up. You're doing nothing more than killing jobs. It's a cemetery for jobs at the E.P.A.

Here is what we know after more than a decade of Republican rule: Texas works. Even 'The New York Times' let it slip into its pages that, 'Texas is the future.'

And I have a message for the liberals and the defenders of the status quo: we're just getting started.

We want taxpayers, not tax wasters.

In the rush to become all things to all people, the federal government has lost sight of its core responsibilities. As a result we're stuck in this frustrating paradox where Washington actually neglects things it's clearly supposed to be doing, while interfering in other areas where they are neither welcome nor authorized.

Texas created more jobs in 2008 than the rest of the states - combined.

Those jobs flee other states because of factors like excessive taxation, punitive regulation and frivolous lawsuits.

Under Obama, our federal tax dollars can now be used to fund abortion all over the world. With the stroke of a pen, abortion essentially became a U.S. foreign export.

Americans want government that is leaner, more efficient, and less intrusive into their personal lives.

Every life is precious.

I think every program needs to stand the sunshine of righteous scrutiny. Whether it's Social Security, whether it's Medicaid, whether it's Medicare.

Let's stand up. Let's speak with pride about our morals and our values and redouble our effort to elect more conservative Republicans.

Our shared conservative values, our belief in the individual is the great hope of our nation.

I've always believed the mission is greater than the man.

Spreading the wealth punishes success while setting America on course for a greater dependency on government.

The Obama administration is an affront to every freedom-loving American, and a threat to every private sector job in this country.

We believe in government involvement that leads to independence: good schools, quality roads and the best health care.

We know there is no such thing as freedom without the risk of failure.

Who can be against progress, after all? But it's a fraudulent use of the word - because for the Progressive, progress is marked not be how free you are, but how much government can 'do' for you.

Democracy functions best when we have an active citizenry.

In Michigan, a liberal democrat raised taxes and kept their government programs at the same level. And guess what? Their economy continued into the toilet, it continued down.

I believe in America. I believe in her purpose and her promise. I believe her best days have not yet been lived. I believe her greatest deeds are reserved for the generations to come.

I mean, Dodd-Frank is strangling small community banks. It doesn't make any difference what the interest rate is. They're not - they're not going to loan the money because they can't make any money for one thing plus the cost of compliance.

I think you need to have a tax system that basically is flat, fair and simple. And - that you can put on a post card. I mean, even Timothy Geithner could do this one and get it on time.

Our party cannot be all things to all people. It can't be. Our loudest opponents on the left are never going to like us so let's stop trying to curry favor with them.

The foundation for future prosperity is built on the bedrock of good jobs and great schools. We are building a strong foundation one job at a time and one educated Texan at a time.

The people who illegally cross into the country are from countries that have very close ties to al Qaeda, whether it's Yemen or Afghanistan, Pakistan, China. It is an absolute national disgrace.

We had a $10 billion budget deficit when we got here in January of 2003. We cut that budget deficit; we did not raise taxes; we came back in '05, and we had an $8 billion surplus. That's how fast it can happen.

According to a study by Achieve Incorporated, Texas is the first state to make a college-prep curriculum the standard coursework in high school, starting with this year's ninth grade class.

And I think most people in this country want to see a president that's got the courage to say we're going to cut the tax burden, and reduce the regulatory climate, and we're going to get Americans working.

Being the Republican front-runner was three of the most exciting hours of my entire life. I've come to grips with it, and the only lasting effect is that I refuse to go on a stage that has more than one podium on it.

I am going to give the American people a huge helping of unbridled truth: that we can't continue to spend what we are spending, that we can't avoid entitlement reform because we are afraid of third rail politics.

I supported Arizona's immigration law by joining in that lawsuit to defend it. Every day I have Texans on that border that are doing their job.

I'm all about job creation. That's what I've done for ten years as the governor of Texas, and that's what I'm focused on.

Our work is before us. It cannot be passed to future legislatures and must not be passed to future generations. May we boldly seize the moment with singular unity. And may we build a Texas of unlimited possibility.

You see, as Americans we're not defined by class, and we will never be told our place. What makes our nation exceptional is that anyone, from any background, can climb the highest of heights.

I'm worried about that man or woman sitting around - the coffee table tonight or in their kitchen talking about how are we going to get to work. How are we going to have the dignity to take care of our family.

I happily cling to my guns and my God, even if President Obama thinks that that is a simpleminded thing in his elitist heart.

I know something. America is not broken, Washington, D.C. is broken.

I got all the respect in the world for the front-runners in this race, but ask yourself: If we replace a Democratic insider with a Republican insider, you think we're really going to change Washington, D.C.? You don't have to settle for Washington and Wall Street insiders who supported the Wall Street bailout and the Obamacare individual mandate.

Our view is that individuals and families can govern their lives better than bureaucrats.

Page one of any economic plan to get America working is to give a pink slip to the current resident in the White House.

We can't have deficit spending in Texas. You have to balance your budget every two years.

Admit it America - 2008 was our national 'oops' moment!

In America, the people are not subjects of government, the government is subject to the people.

It is through states that the American people get the job done every day, often in spite of a deeply flawed bureaucratic federal government.

It's time to bring tough medicine to Washington. No longer will policy be set by K Street, it will be dictated by Main Street.

Our goal is to displace the entrenched powers in Washington, restore the rightful balance between the state and federal government.

I learned that not everyone values life like we do in America, or the rights that are endowed to every human being by a loving God.

Let's make what Americans buy. Buy what Americans make. And sell it to the world.

My hope is that that person will come forward that can win the presidency that we can all get behind.

When the good lord calls you home, the government ought not come get your home.

This administration in Washington that's in power now clearly believes that government is not only the answer to every need, but it's the most qualified to make the most central decisions for every American in every area.

President Obama's call for nearly a half-trillion dollars in more government stimulus when America has more than $14 trillion in debt is guided by his mistaken belief that we can spend our way to prosperity.

I disagree with the concept that somehow or another we're going to pack up 10, to 12, to 15 million people and ship them back to the country of origin. That's not going to happen.

We've got the wind at our back right now. Americans are waking up to the realities of their previous choices. We must keep America moving back to preeminence because our values and conservative ideas are the world's greatest hope.

It is up to us, to this present generation of Americans, to take a stand for freedom, to send a message to Washington that we're taking our future back from the grips of central planners who would control our healthcare, who would spend our treasure, who downgrade our future and micro-manage our lives.

Texas has long been known as the nation's largest energy producer, but we are equally proud of our distinction as the nation's leading energy innovator.

We stand up and proudly proclaim that Washington is not our caretaker and we reject a state, in Margaret Thatcher's words, a state that takes too much from us to do too much for us.

Marco Rubio

The American Dream is a term that is often used but also often misunderstood. It isn't really about becoming rich or famous. It is about things much simpler and more fundamental than that.

You cannot give up on the American dream. We cannot allow our fears and our disappointments to lead us into silence and into inaction.

The Hispanic community understands the American Dream and have not forgotten what they were promised - that in the U.S., a free market system, allows us all to succeed economically, achieve stability and security for your family and leave your children better off than yourselves.

We live in a society obsessed with public opinion. But leadership has never been about popularity.

We don't need new taxes. We need new taxpayers, people that are gainfully employed, making money and paying into the tax system. And then we need a government that has the discipline to take that additional revenue and use it to pay down the debt and never grow it again.

Leadership can not be measured in a poll or even in the result of an election. It can only be truly seen with the benefit of time. From the perspective of 20 years, not 20 days.

Our problem with President Obama isn't that he's a bad person. By all accounts, he too is a good husband, and a good father - and thanks to lots of practice, a pretty good golfer.

Every single one of us is the descendant of a go-getter. Of dreamers and of believers.

Let us agree here today to adopt among ourselves a simple and unwritten rule. We will not rise to criticize someone else's idea unless we are prepared to offer an alternative idea of our own.

My parents were working class folks. My dad was a bartender for most of his life, my mom was a maid and a cashier and a stock clerk at WalMart. We were not people of financial means in terms of significant financial means. I always told them, 'I didn't always have what I wanted. I always had what I needed.' My parents always provided that.

Our national motto is 'In God we Trust,' reminding us that faith in our Creator is the most important American value of all.

For those who aspire to live in a high cost, high tax, big government place, our nation and the world offers plenty of options. Vermont, Canada and Venezuela all offer you the opportunity to live in the socialist, big government paradise you long for.

This is the only country in the world where today's employee, is tomorrow's employer.

They made it to the middle class, my dad working as a bartender and my mother as a cashier and a maid. I didn't inherit any money from them. But I inherited something far better - the real opportunity to accomplish my dreams.

America is the story of everyday people who did extraordinary things. A story woven deep into the fabric of our society.

I'm theologically in line with the Roman Catholic Church. I believe in the authority of the church, but I also have tremendous respect for my brothers and sisters in other Christian faiths.

Conservatism is not about leaving people behind. Conservatism is about empowering people to catch up, to give them the tools at their disposable that make it possible for them to access all the hope, all the promise, all the opportunity that America offers. And our programs to help them should reflect that.

The way to turn our economy around is not by making rich people poorer, it's by making poor people richer.

You cannot do anything without God. It's a profound and elemental truth. Not, you cannot do most things without God. You will not be able to do anything that you want, truly, in fulfillment, without God.

I would love nothing more than compromise. But I would say to you that compromise that's not a solution is a waste of time.

From tea parties to the election in Massachusetts, we are witnessing the single greatest political pushback in American history.

The president we have today is a typical Washington politician that's prone to hyperbole and decisiveness and false outrage. And I think it's very sad - very sad to watch.

I traveled the state of Florida for two years campaigning. I have never met a job creator who told me that they were waiting for the next tax increase before they started growing their business. I've never met a single job creator who's ever said to me I can't wait until government raises taxes again so I can go out and create a job.

The Second Amendment is a constitutional right. I didn't make it up, the Republican Party didn't make it up. It's in the Constitution. I think it's just as important as any of the other rights in our constitution.

How come liberals never admit that they're liberal? They've now come up with a new word called 'progressive,' which I thought was an insurance company but apparently it's a label.

Do not be afraid to offer ideas that draw opposition. Remember, if no one is against your idea, then your idea probably doesn't do anything.

The No. 1 issue in the Hispanic American community is 'How do I leave my children better off than myself?

Free enterprise makes people prosperous, all people prosperous, and big government makes people poorer.

We've never been people that go around and confront people that have been financially successful and say, 'We hate you. We envy you because of how well you're doing.'

We need transparency in government spending. We need to put each government expenditure online so every Floridian can see where their tax money is being spent.

These terrorists aren't trying to kill us because we offended them. They attack us because they want to impose their view of the world on as many people as they can, and America is standing in their way.

Americans chose a limited government that exists to protect our rights, not to grant them.

We cannot allow our fears and our disappointments to lead us into silence and into inaction. Because this country that God has blessed us with, it is worth fighting for.

Americans chose a free enterprise system designed to provide a quality of opportunity, not compel a quality of results. And that is why this is only place in the world where you can open up a business in the spare bedroom of your home.

My dad was a bartender. My mom was a cashier, a maid and a stock clerk at K-Mart. They never made it big. They were never rich. And yet they were successful. Because just a few decades removed from hopelessness, they made possible for us all the things that had been impossible for them.

The idea that more taxes and more government spending is the best way to help hardworking middle class taxpayers - that's an old idea that's failed every time it's been tried.

I think there are some in the Democratic Party - not all - but I think there are some people in the Democratic Party that think that the immigration issue is more valuable to them unsolved. That it gives them something to talk about, that they can go back to Hispanic communities and make unrealistic promises every two years and win votes.

Supporting the definition of marriage as one man and one woman is not anti-gay: it is pro-traditional marriage. And if support for traditional marriage is bigotry, then Barack Obama was a bigot until just before the 2012 election.

We should be the pro-legal immigration party. A party that has a positive platform and agenda on how we can create a legal immigration system that works for immigrants and works for America.

What is the conservative movement? It's pretty straightforward. We believe that the way prosperity is created is when people have the freedom and the opportunity to pursue their dreams.

Let me start by saying that I do not enjoy nor relish the partisan role of attack dog. I never found any fun in that. I don't think it's constructive. I don't intend to become that here in the Senate.

We can't stop talking about the importance of our values and our culture. We can't stop talking about them because the moral well-being of our people is directly linked to their economic well-being.

Big government helps the people who have made it. It doesn't help the people who are trying to make it; it crushes the people who are trying to make it.

That thought process that somehow other people have to be worse off in order for you to be better off does not work. People get on boats people jump fences to get away from that kind of thought process.

If you're the cashier at Burger King, of course you make less than the manager or even the CEO. The issue is whether you're stuck being a cashier for the rest of your life.

Never has the political class or the mainstream media that covers them been more out of touch with the American people than they are today.

The second truism that we must understand is that poverty does not create our social problems, our social problems create our poverty.

Conservatism has always been about reforming government and solving problems, and that's why the conservative movement should lead on immigration reform.

I don't ever remember them telling us or teaching us that the only way we could be more successful is if other people were less successful. They never inculcated the belief that somehow, in order for us to climb the ladder, other people have to come down from the ladder.

No community values entrepreneurship and small business more than the Hispanic community.

You know what the fastest growing religion in America is? Statism. The growing reliance on government.

Unlike any other leader in modern American history, we are led today by a president that has decided to pit Americans against each other.

You know that big government doesn't hurt big corporations. They've got the best lawyers and accountants in the world. You know who gets destroyed by big government? It's the little guys.

We focus so much on how immigrants can change America that we forget that

America has always changed immigrants even more.

The Democrats never fight about who is more like Jimmy Carter.

We need to make sure our government programs encourage work, not dependence.

Hope and Change has become Divide and Conquer.

Our people want jobs. They don't want a safety net as a way of life.

A key part of your sovereignty is the ability to control the influx and outflow of your people and is the ability to secure your border.

Che Guevara was a racist.

For many of us who were born and raised in this country, including me, it's sometimes easy to forget how special America really is.

When was the last time you heard news accounts of a boatload of American refugees arrive on the shores of another country?

And yet, there are still people in American politics who, for some reason, cling to this belief that America is better off adopting the economic policies of nations whose people who immigrate here from there.

But America was founded on the principle that every person has God-given rights. That power belongs to the people. That government exists to protect our rights and serve our interests. That we shouldn't be trapped in the circumstances of our birth. That we should be free to go as far as our talents and work can take us.

But here's what I would tell people of my generation. I turn 40 this year. There isn't going to be a Social Security. There isn't going to be a Medicare when you retire.

Forget about what your benefit is going to look like. There isn't going to be one if we don't make some reforms to save that program now.

But let me tell you what happens when regulations go too far, when they seem to exist only for the purpose of justifying the existence of a regulator. It kills the people trying to start a business.

We must educate and train our children to compete and succeed in the 21st century. Our kids are not going to grow up to compete with children in Alabama or Mississippi. They're going to grow up to compete with kids in India, and China, all over the world; children who are learning to compete and succeed in the 21st century themselves.

Presidents in both parties - from John F. Kennedy to Ronald Reagan - have known that our free-enterprise economy is the source of our middle-class prosperity.

We are a nation of haves and soon-to-haves, of people who have made it and people who will make it. And that's who we need to remain.

I think there is a real misunderstanding about what the Tea Party movement is. The Tea Party movement is a sentiment in America that government is broken - both parties are to blame - and if we don't do something soon, this exceptional country will be lost, and it will become just like everybody else.

It's easier to sell cotton candy than it is to sell broccoli to somebody, but the broccoli is better for you, and the same thing with a limited government.

Regulation is necessary to protect our natural environment, keep our food and medicine safe, and ensure fair competition and fair treatment of our workers.

The conservative movement is about government playing its important yet limited role, and about not falling into the trap of believing that every problem has an exclusive government answer for it.

Thousands of years of human history have shown that the ideal setting for children to grow up is with a mother and a father committed to one another, living together, and sharing the responsibility of raising their children.

You know who a complicated tax code kills? The guy or gal trying to start a business out of the spare bedroom of their home. So we've got to simplify our tax code.

If my house was on fire, I can't compromise about which part of the house I'm going to save. You save the whole house or it will all burn down. We either save this country or we do not.

I'm proud of the fact that the Republican Party is the pro-life party on the issue of life.

But those who believe that what our people desire is big government are living in a state of delusion.

We Americans are as great as we have ever been. But our government is broken.

The problem is that when government controls the economy, those who can influence government keep winning, and everybody else just stays the same.

Anyone who doesn't agree with the Left's approach to immigration oftentimes gets stigmatized as anti-immigrant or anti-Hispanic.

Big government doesn't help the middle class, it buries it.

Criminals don't care what the law is.

For most of history, almost everyone was poor. Power and wealth belonged to only a few.

I have never voted for a tax increase.

Minimum wage laws have never worked in terms of having the middle class attain more prosperity.

No one is in favor of a bill that would force American citizens to have to interact with law enforcement in a way that wasn't appropriate.

Raising taxes won't create private sector jobs.

What happens across the planet can have a greater impact on your family than what happens down the street.

I am prepared to discuss the things that I believe we need to do not just to raise the debt limit. Raising the debt limit is the easiest thing. That's one vote away. The hard thing is to show the world we are serious about putting our spending in order so we can show people we'll able to pay our bills down the road.

Tim Scott

There are good people and bad people in all organizations fundamentally however, when you look at the basis of the Tea Party it has nothing to do with race. It has to do with an economic recovery. It has to do with limiting the role of our government in our lives. It has to do with free markets.

I think one of the most threatening places to be in politics is a black conservative because there are so many liberals who want to continue to reinforce a stereotype that doesn't exist about America.

We need the private sector to create jobs. If the government could create jobs Communism would have worked, but it didn't.

As a small business owner for the last 15 years, when I think of what truly changed my life, it was my faith, a strong family, my mom did a really, really good job of encouraging me in very clear and discernible ways.

I know that my grandfather is 92 years old. And he has seen this country evolve in amazing ways. He looks at South Carolina and he says, wow, what an amazing state that we have the blessing to live within because of the evolution.

There is nothing special about Tim Scott. I'm an ordinary guy serving an extraordinary God and that makes the difference.

I have campaigned all over the state of South Carolina. It is the friendliest state in the country. And truly here people judge you by the content of your character not the color of your skin.

Certainly I feel like I'm the tip of the arrow at times because certainly the national media wants to talk about the fact that I'm a black Republican and some people think of that as zany that a black person would be a conservative but to me what is zany is any person black, white, red, brown or yellow not being a conservative.

I think the question is who am I? That's what we all should be asking ourselves. Who am I? Well, if I am first a Christian conservative then that dictates my response to all questions so my response first as a Christian conservative is to vote consistent with my value system.

I'm not looking to be dominating all the media outlets ... to talk about any issue just to be on TV, I'm not your guy. I'm not going to be 'the black Republican'. I'm going to be a Republican who happens to be black who will talk about issues that I'm passionate about that are specific to the agenda that I want to accomplish.

Ensuring fairness in the American workplace should be a cornerstone of our economic policy.

South Carolina is a great place to be from.

But the question we should ask ourselves is, who is the next visionary leader of America? How do we have the aspiration and inspire Americans to reach their highest level? We need a president that does so.

If our message reaches the kitchen tables, we are in good shape.

If the small government concept grows, we have fewer dollars leaving our pockets, we have more folks motivated to make a profit.

I think it's very clear that the American people are frustrated with this move toward socialism. And so whether you're back or white, if you believe that the conservative construct is in the best interest of our future, than you too would be voting with Republicans, and if you had the opportunity to run you'd join us as well.

And the Tea Party represents many of us who believe that we are taxed enough already. We believe in free markets.

I'm an ordinary guy serving an extraordinary God - and that makes the difference.

I'm going to be a Republican who happens to be black - who will talk about issues that I'm passionate about.

If Strom Thurmond could get 30% of the black vote, any Republican can.

We have to attack those things which stand in the way of America progress. And what stands in the way of American progress right now is the federal government.

Success is created in studio apartments and garages, at kitchen tables, and in classrooms across the nation, not in government conference rooms in Washington.

Thousands of Americans are forced to join unions as a condition of employment, with little to no chance of ever having their voices heard.

I failed world geography, civics, Spanish and English. And when you fail Spanish and English, they do not consider you bilingual. They may call you bi-ignorant because you can't speak any language.

I remember walking down the aisle, and I got down on my knees as a person who is so selfish, but when I rose back up the Lord had become the Master of my life.

If you look at the fact that the best chance we have for a good economy is the private sector. The government cannot create jobs. If the government could create jobs, then Communism would have worked. But didn't work. So what we have to do is allow the private sector and the entrepreneurial spirit to lead us back to a job-filled recovery.

The first time that I was elected I was called the Judas Iscariot of the black community because I took a stand that was inconsistent of cutting across the grain.

When I was in the 9th grade I was flunking out of high school. And that's why I'm so encouraged by the fact that America is the place where opportunity and American exceptionalism is alive and well.

Obamacare. Get rid of it. Period.

The future of the Republican Party and the future of America is based on a values system and the issues that drive those values are on our side.

I think you hear, at least as an undertone, and it's going to grow louder, is that we believe that capitalism is the mantra of the day and anything that creeps towards socialism is a problem.

We do not have a revenue problem in D.C. or this county. We have a prioritization problem. When you create the priorities you fund the priorities of the country and you stop spending money when you get to zero.

As I have traveled throughout my Congressional district, the one thing I heard loud and clear was simply please stop spending money you do not have, rein in spending, live within a budget.

People ask me about if, being a Republican, you guys want to cut everything and stop everything and not help people. I find that patently false.

I was warmly embraced by the Tea Party. They openly seek more minorities.

Starting and feeding into the cultural war is absolutely unequivocally wrong for us as a nation and bad for the conservative movement.

But in my life, the vast majority of people that have really afforded me the opportunity to succeed were white folks.

I believe Americans have a strong work ethic.

I think about my grandfather who's 89 years old, and the last thing he needs is more money out of his pocket.

I think when you look to the future what you'll find is that the Republican Party is building a bigger party base on stronger values.

Our position should not be on how to eliminate the competition at all expenses, but we should focus on what we're going to do in order to make sure that Americans turn to the road of prosperity with the trajectory of capitalism, because making a profit is not an evil.

I don't necessarily believe there's a message in the fact that I'm an African-American Republican. I think there is a message that America as a whole, we are now awake. We are looking at a political construct and we're fairly disappointed. I think the message is no matter where you come from in this country, there is great potential.

I just dove into the Scriptures and started memorizing different scriptures and started becoming as much as possible a part of the scripture. I wanted it to be grafted into my heart.

I see myself as a person who wants to serve the constituents within my district and find a way to move those who are not in our position philosophically to our position.

Part of the challenge of being a black Republican anywhere is that you start off with people walking in with chips on their shoulder trying to figure out what is wrong with you.

Scott Walker

Let this be our time in history so that someday we can tell our children and grandchildren that we were there, that we changed the course of history for the better.

The unions say 'last hired - first fired,', we say hire and fire based on merit. We want the best and brightest in the classroom.

I think in the end the big issue is that the private sector still needs more help. And the answer is not more big government. I know in my state our reforms allowed us to protect firefighters, police officers, and teachers.

Political leaders in Illinois kicked the can down the road, raised taxes, and ignored fiscal realities. Now, they're realizing the consequences of their actions: credit downgrades and negative outlooks.

Political leaders in Illinois kicked the can down the road, raised taxes, and ignored fiscal realities. Now, they're realizing the consequences of their actions: credit downgrades and negative outlooks.

It's time to put our differences aside and find ways to work together to move Wisconsin forward.

I've often heard the complaint from both Democrat and Republican voters alike that they hate the fact that politicians get into office and they - and they're fearful, they're fearful to make tough decisions because they think more about the next election than they do about the next-generation.

But I don't want massive layoffs of anyone - public or private. We are planning on shrinking government through attrition and reform, not through random pink slips.

What has made America amazing has been the fact that throughout our history, throughout the more than 200 years of our history, there have been men and women of courage who stood up and decided it was more important to look out for the future of their children and their grandchildren than their own political futures.

Who is in charge? Is it taxpayers or is it the special interest groups?

I kept my promises.

Elections have consequences.

In education, they say either property taxes have to go up, or we'll have poor education - that's a false choice.

I hate big government, but I really hate a government that doesn't work. So when 'they say we either have to raise taxes or cut core services,' it's actually a 'false choice.'

My problem with public sector union leaders, the bosses, has been they stood in the way of protecting the taxpayer.

Looking at America's history, ordinary people did something extraordinary. Leaders risked their lives for freedoms that we take for granted today. That's what instills confidence. That's us. We will move forward and prosper because that's who we are as Americans.

My kids were targeted on Facebook by protesters.

People create jobs, not the government.

There could not be a more stark contrast between Wisconsin and Illinois.

We showed that when we say 'Wisconsin is open for business', we mean it.

You can make tough decisions that I believe voters for years have asked us to do.

Certainly political capital-slash-celebrity attention, whatever you want to call it, certainly is part of the reason why I've been reaching out to CEOs. There's a lot of folks who probably would have taken a call from me before but are even more inclined now and are interested in what we're doing because of all the attention.

I believe that smaller government is better government. But I also believe that in the areas where government does play a legitimate role, we should demand that it is done better.

But Mitt Romney understands, like I understand, that people - not governments - create jobs.

So why am I facing a recall election? Simple: the big government union bosses from Washington want their money. They don't like the fact that I did something fundamentally pro-worker; something that's truly about freedom.

A wise governor told me a long time ago, political capital you don't get more of by keeping it. You get it by using it.

You've got to have a vision. You've got to have a message.

Now things have changed for the better. Our reforms end seniority and tenure so we can hire and fire based on merit and pay based on performance. That means we can put the best and the brightest in our classrooms - and we can keep them there.

And I think Governor Romney has a shot if the 'R' next to his name doesn't just stand for 'Republican,' it stands for 'reformer.'

I promised to empower the taxpayer - instead of a handful of big government union bosses.

One of those promises was to limit the size of government and to have the government serve the people - and not the other way around.

So let me be clear, Collective bargaining isn't a right, it is an expensive entitlement. Once and for all, we are giving the taxpayers a voice in this debate. We put the power back in the hands of the people.

When we win, it will tell every politician in America that if you are bold, if you do the right thing, if you tackle the tough issues, there will be people standing there right with you.

I think most people believe success in government is how many fewer people are in government, not because you kick them off of benefits like unemployment but they've been able to control their own destiny because private sector employers have created more jobs.

It is only fair to expect public employees like me and others in the public sector to pay something close to what our neighbors and our fellow citizens do in the private sector.

More people on unemployment benefits is not success in America, fewer people on not because we kicked them off but because they have been able to get a job in the private sector, because government got out of the way.

We are the ones looking out for the middle class. Who do think pays for the endless expansion of government? Its middle class taxpayers. Our reforms protect middle class taxpayers.

What makes America amazing is that there have always been men and women of courage who were willing to think more about the future of their children and grandchildren than they did about their own political careers.

You look at Governor Romney's record in the private sector, he helped turn businesses around. Certainly a decade ago he took what would have been an international disaster with the U.S. Olympics, and turned it around for America and made us great again with the Olympics in Salt Lake City.

We could see the Teamsters coming in from New Jersey, the AFL-CIO from Chicago. You could see all of the people being bused in.

Mitt Romney turned businesses around in the private sector. He saved the Winter Olympics.

I have not made any plans for the future, and my wife would kill me if I announced anything before that.

I joke with my kids, who love history, that I'll be the only governor to be elected twice in his first term.

I'd like now and into the future to play a bigger role not only in Wisconsin and the Midwest, but nationally. I'd like to have an impact.

One of the things I get amused by is when my opponent talks about the middle class.

The real bottom line is, the national unions want their hands on the money.

We need someone to turn things around in America.

We'll look to the fall and if there is a new president and a new Senate that's part of a

Congress willing to change, that's the next step.